Fluent in French:
The most complete study guide to learn French

Frederic Bibard
(talkinfrench.com)

Table of Contents

ACKNOWLEDGEMENTS

I WOULD LIKE TO EXPRESS MY GRATITUDE TO THE MANY PEOPLE WHO SAW ME THROUGH THIS BOOK; TO ALL THOSE WHO PROVIDED SUPPORT, TALKED THINGS OVER, READ, WROTE, OFFERED COMMENTS, ALLOWED ME TO QUOTE THEIR REMARKS AND ASSISTED IN THE EDITING, PROOFREADING AND DESIGN.

I want to thank my mother, my father and the rest of my family, who supported and encouraged me in spite of all the time it took me away from them.

I would like to thank Catherine, Janey, Lauren, Helen for enabling me to publish this book.

Thanks to Wesley, Kimberly, Catherine and other students. Without you this book would be very different.

INTRODUCTION

You know as well as I do that learning French can be quite difficult. Adding to the degree of difficulty is the fact that, in each direction you look, you are bombarded with a deluge of French learning resources. *So the questions arise.*

What is the best learning method to use?
Which will work best for my motivation type and level of learning?
Where exactly should I begin?

Throughout my years of teaching French, I have heard these dilemmas over and over again, from hundreds of French learners. When not done properly, learning a new language can be *pull-your-hair-out* frustrating. When you do not know which way to look, it can be overwhelming at best and miserable at worst.

Even as I say this, you are probably wondering, *"Out of the many available resources in the market and all of the different methods claiming to be the best way to learn French, why exactly should I pick this book?"*

There are many things I could say about what this study guide *is*, but let me tell you what it is *not*.

It is NOT your usual run-of-the-mill study guide

I created this book specifically with learners like you in mind. When I first began teaching French in 2008, I was amazed (and deeply troubled) by the dearth of good quality resources that resonate fully with different kinds of learners. Yes, there are plenty of good books on the subject, but I was looking for something different, something the average learner could relate to. I wanted something not for only beginners, but something that those from all different backgrounds, and varying levels can learn from

Sounds ambitious? Probably. But if you cannot find the material you're looking for, the best way to solve the problem is to create the material yourself....so that's exactly what I did!

This study guide is designed and crafted with the needs of learners in mind, and the result of the years of conversations with French learners like you.

This is NOT a band-aid solution to learning the language

While there are no shortcuts or quick fixes to learning French, this book offers tried-and-tested tips that will help you navigate your way towards your goal. It provides practical advice on habit-creation and how to maintain your motivation, busts long-held myths about learning languages, shares brilliant ideas for improving listening skills and pronunciation, lists tips for getting the best out of reading in French, and gives clear-cut guidelines for writing in French like an expert. This book is brimming with sure-fire ways to boost your French studies.

Learning French may not be easy, but this book will help you work your way around the pitfalls and difficulties of language-learning until you reach fluency.

This will NOT be a one-shot deal

The study guide is only the beginning – and it is the perfect starting point for you no matter which age bracket you belong to or what your background and level of learning are. When you purchase this book, you also get a special bonus – a-step-by-step learning plan catered specifically to your individual learning needs. Think of it as something resembling a healthy meal plan designed for your nutritional requirements. As your go-to guy for learning French, I also have loads of other resources that you can use when you head over to my website, www.talkinfrench.com.

So, what are you waiting for? Let's get started!

Chapter 1 –
Motivation and Habit

Motivation

Motivation is not a one-size-fits-all package deal, especially when it comes to learning French. Anyone who chooses to study this language has his or her own individual reasons for it. Think about the reason you have chosen to learn French. Perhaps it is for school or university. Some people learn it for work purposes. Others are inspired to learn French for traveling or pleasure. Many people have a genuine interest in the French culture, food, sports or lifestyle and are motivated to learn the language because of these factors.

Regardless of the reason you are learning French, you will need to study and focus to successfully gain skills for understanding a second language. It is not an easy task, and motivation to continue learning will not come out of the blue. Staying motivated to learn French is not as simple as having a structured study schedule, either. It is, and should be, more in-depth than staring at a textbook during your study time and waiting for fluency to come to you.

Your motivation to learn French needs to be exciting, inspiring, and relevant. This is often the case when you begin to learn French. Many people, for example, commit to learning the language as a New Year's Resolution. Yet, after the 'honeymoon' period of taking up French, they reach a point where they must put in more effort to progress forward. This is where motivation begins to slip away.

By taking the following points into account, you can discover new ways to maintain your motivation for learning French.

Passion

Passion is just the thing you need to kick start your motivation. Without passion, the process of moving forward with learning French will become a struggle. Think back to high school, for example, when you were taking compulsory subjects that were part of the curriculum. There is likely one subject that you felt very little enthusiasm for and therefore you dreaded going to the class. Doing homework for this subject was a struggle, and staying focused on the content was a challenge, right? This is common when you do not feel passionate about a topic.

The same goes for learning a second language. If you feel that French is an obligation, something you *must* do rather than something you *want* to do, motivation will be harder to achieve. The key to overcoming this is finding your passion. You can do this by drawing inspiration from your everyday life.

The following examples demonstrate ways you can turn your interests or hobbies into a French learning experience:

Are you a sports fanatic, a music lover, an artist extraordinaire, a cooking enthusiast, a bookworm, or a film aficionado? See how you can capitalize on your interests to cultivate your motivation for learning French.

- Sports fanatic: Watch a sports game with French commentary, or read sports reports in French. Visit the website http://www.lequipe.fr/ for sources.

- Music lover: Listen to some French music. If you play an instrument, try to learn a few French songs. I have shared a playlist of more than 600 songs on my website, which you can check out here. You can listen to the music for free, but if you cannot access the playlist, try the website: deezer.

- Artist extraordinaire: Look up famous French artists, both historical and contemporary, and read more about their works and lives in France. I recommend listening to France Culture. They have a podcast and a show dedicated to these things. Plus, they speak clear and distinct French.

- Cooking enthusiast: Become a French master chef by cooking traditional meals and desserts while reading the recipes in French. If you enjoy French foods but your French is not quite there yet, check out the blog of David Leboviz. If you already have a decent grasp of French, try the website Marmitton, which boasts a collection of more than 6,000 recipes.

- Book worm: Instead of picking up a book in your first language, challenge yourself by reading one in French.

    If you are in an early stage of learning, I suggest referring to eBooks with an English Glossary. A few options include: books by Sylvie Lainé., an eBook I have created called "Learn French with 7 stories," or, if you prefer something longer but without a glossary, you can try "Pauvre Anne." You can also try to read novels in Easy French (Français Facile). I recommend that you check online, specifically, CLE - International Publisher, for options.

    For intermediate-level learners, check out Le petit prince, Le petit Nicolas, and l'étranger. These are very popular titles and they are not too complicated.

    More advanced learners can try Anna Gavalda, Amélie Nothomb or Guillaume Musso.

> For even more resources, check out an article related to this topic on my website, talkinfrench.com.

- Film aficionado: Play a French movie and enjoy some great cinematography while improving your listening fluency. On my website, you can find a list of movies and where to watch them online. Do not hesitate to have a look! Some examples can be found here.

> Need more resources? Check out the resource section at the end of this book.

Whatever your hobbies and interests in life may be, you can use them to encourage yourself to make progress with French. These are the things you should turn to when you find yourself struggling for motivation.

Immersion

Immersion works because it plays off of your interests and passions, which we now know are highly pivotal to successfully learning French.

Instead of obligating yourself to study for a solid two hours each day, try an alternative structure. Consider watching a French movie, listening to some French songs, or reading a recipe in French. Doing these little things throughout the week, as well as studying for a solid period when you have time and the right mind set, will produce a higher-quality French learning experience.

Variety

Keep in mind that there is not just one form of motivation. Likewise, you should not feel obligated to stick to one pattern of motivation. If you find yourself becoming motivated for a different reason than the one you started with, it is completely fine. As you progress with French, you will find new things to motivate you and uncover previously unknown interests and passions within your learning process.

There are two main forms of motivation and each serves a different purpose. These are essentially motivational "umbrellas," and under each umbrella are different processes and formulas for motivational success.

- Integrative motivation: Motivation for something with the purpose of immersion. This occurs when learning French is motivated by the desire to live or travel in a French-speaking country or to be immersed wholly in the French culture.

- Instrumental motivation: Motivation derived from prac- tical or pragmatic purposes. Perhaps you need French courses to complete your school or university studies, or knowing the language will aid in gaining a job or a promotion.

Both forms of motivation are valid when learning French as a second language. If you take a job in a French speaking country, for example, both forms of motivation will be at play. The inte- grative motivation may make you socially outgoing because of your desire to be integrated with French speakers. Meanwhile, the instrumental motivation may cause you to focus on grammar and spelling so that you can read and write effectively for work. By allowing both types of motivations to work in tandem, you will open yourself to finding encouragement to learn French in differ- ent ways and for different purposes.

Quality vs. Quantity

You want to learn French and you want to learn it well. Un- derstanding a second language requires time, commitment, and dedication. As you begin learning French, your enthusiasm lev- els are high and these factors seem easy to maintain. As reality catches up to you, however, and you find yourself struggling with the commitment of learning French, motivation begins to fade away.

The key to learning French is quality over quantity. It may feel productive to set the goal of studying French for two hours every day, but it is not the most beneficial approach for two reasons:

1. Time-frame goals are not specific enough
2. Two hours a day is not realistic or achievable for most people

The likely outcome if you use this method is, for the first two days, you will study for the two hours you assigned yourself. Come day three and onwards, you will realize that real life gets in the way of this two hour time block. By the time you finish with work, going to the gym, cooking dinner, spending time with your family, walking the dog, doing the housework, or whatever your circumstances require, you will find that there are not enough hours in the day to stick to your study goals. But because you are determined to study for those two hours every day, you cram it in right before bedtime. So it is 11:30 at night and you open up your textbook. Your eyes start drooping, you stifle a yawn, and your focus fades rapidly. What is the quality of study *really* going to be like at this point?

For the best results when learning French, time is the key: time to learn, time for the information to be absorbed, and time for your brain to rest. Rather than forcing yourself to study at a time when your brain is not really up for it, wait until you are genuinely interested in the work in front of you. Even if this means only studying from your textbook for an hour and a half on a Saturday morning, the information you absorb during this time will be of much higher quality.

This approach may cause you to feel as if you are not investing enough time in learning French. However, this is not necessarily the case. Formal studying is not the only way to learn French. Studying the grammar rules, verb conjugations and sentence structures need to be complemented with other forms of learning. As we will discuss in the next section of this chapter, immersion is a highly effective way to learn French.

Positive Associations

There is a lot to be said for the power of positive thinking. The moment learning French becomes an awful obligation, take it as a warning sign to act quickly and reclaim your motivation. This can be easily avoided by creating positive associations with learning French. There are two types of motivation we will focus on: *Intrinsic motivation* and *extrinsic motivation*

Intrinsic motivation

Intrinsic motivation occurs when learning French makes you feel good about yourself. It is an entirely personal and internal motivation in which you desire to make progress with something, in this case learning French, for immaterial purposes. Being able to speak, read, and write in another language is a great way to boost your confidence to a whole other level. If being able to speak a new sentence in French or understand new vocabulary makes you proud of yourself, hold on to this feeling and allow it to become your motivation. Learning French is difficult; do not be afraid to pat yourself on the back and feel wonderful for achieving new things.

Extrinsic motivation

Sometimes, the good feeling we get when we accomplish something just is not enough. Extrinsic motivation is when we are encouraged to be motivated by an external source. This might be a reward in the form of your favourite food or going out with friends on the weekend. If you are struggling with motivation to learn French, it can be effective to have a rewards system. For example, if you have a test in class, your extrinsic motivation is to get the best grade possible. Your reward for getting the good grade might be a bottle of quality French champagne. The grade is your external motivation while the reward is something enticing to further this motivation. This can also be an excellent way to celebrate your achievements as they happen.

Resources

One reason many people lose motivation when learning French is the common conception that it is too difficult. The thought of learning French can be intimidating compared to the idea of learning English. This is not because English is an easier language; rather, the perception is that there are more resources available for English learners than there are for French learners

In reality, there are many great resources available for speaking, reading, and writing French. With these fantastic resources at hand, you will have some great reference points to utilize when you need some extra motivation to stay focused.

At the end of this eBook, I will share a boatload of resources (free and paid) to help you learn French.

Habit: The Most Important Element in Learning

The general rule for habits is that it takes several weeks (between three and six weeks, according to some studies) for an action to become a habit. When turning something into a habit, the first two weeks are the easiest. This is the period where you are most motivated and eager to progress with this action. However, the final week of creating a habit can be a struggle. While this is the most crucial point, it is also the point when the action becomes the most difficult to maintain. Regarding learning French, the final weeks may be the point when you do not feel you are making much progress or you hit your first real challenge. The final weeks of creating a habit are when your motivation is most likely to decline.

Habits in the Long Term

In order to keep your motivation levels high, it is important to think ahead. Habits need long-term relevance. If you are trying to create a habit without thinking of how it is going to impact your future, it is easy to stop the action after three weeks and lose the habit altogether.

In order to successfully create a habit of learning French, you must ask yourself the following questions:

- How will I continue this habit in the future?
- What will the long-term benefit of this habit be?
- How will I maintain the habit over a month-long period?

Habits vs. Goals

When you are learning French, your immediate reaction might be to set goals for yourself. Goals make sense because they are achievements that you can tick off as you progress. However, goals are not the solution to maintaining your motivation for learning French. Goals tend to put the focus on the end results of a process, but **it is the process that is the most important part.** The process of learning French is the time during which you discover new interests related to the French language. If you are too busy focusing on the end goal, you can overlook these discoveries.

The process of learning French is fantastic because it is fluid. When you learn something new, it causes you to ask other questions, and, suddenly, you are heading in a different direction of learning because of something you were interested in during the process. This is where including every day habits of practicing French in your life is much more productive than waiting for a goal to be achieved.

Let's say, for example, that your habit is to read a French blog or newspaper during your lunch break at work. While reading this blog, you find some new vocabulary. You are not sure what a certain phrase means, so you look it up and find the translation. The phrase sticks in your mind because you found it interesting and you remember the sentence you read it in. The next time you are writing a letter or an essay in French, you use the phrase or the sentence because you remember how good it sounded.

Learning a new word or expression might not have been a goal you set for yourself, but because the process of learning French is a habit for you, you have inadvertently soaked up new and valuable information that enhances your French knowledge. Not only do you now have a different way of expressing yourself in French, but you have also likely read some interesting information in the blog or newspaper. This is a productive habit.

Habits for Easy Goals, Intensity for Hard Goals

While habits have excellent long-term benefits, they are best used for the easy elements of learning French. The "easy" things tend to be things we find most interesting, such as listening to French music or reading a blog on an interesting topic. However, it is important not to neglect the difficult elements of learning French. These include tedious tasks such as learning grammar and pronunciation.

When you start off learning French and creating these habits throughout the learning process, you are filled with enthusiasm and motivation. As we have acknowledged, maintaining this motivation can be a challenge. However, its presence for the short term can be used as an effective drive to create goals.

There are certain things you need to understand about French right at the beginning of your learning journey in order to progress successfully. This is where short term, high intensity goals come in. The early stage of learning French is the ideal time to set a solid foundation. Here are some examples of high intensity goals:

- Perfect your pronunciation for words that have silent

letters or difficult vowel sounds.
- Memorize irregular verb conjugations for irregular verbs, such as être, aller, faire and avoir.
- Gain a solid understanding of accents.
- Memorize masculine and feminine word endings.

Everyday Immersion

Habits are, essentially, things that you do each day. Over the course of time, they become permanent features of your everyday routine. This is why creating a habit of doing something pertaining to learning French each day is an effective way to learn the language. Once French becomes a habit for you, it will become rare that you do not think, speak, or read in French every day.

Here are some examples of how you can include French in your everyday routine:

- Listen to a French podcast during your commute to work
- Read a French blog while eating breakfast or on your lunch break
- Watch a funny French video on YouTube while waiting for your dinner to cook
- Listen to French music while working out at the gym or going for a run
- Unload the dishwasher and say the French word for the items as you put them away
- Label your house with French words for objects in each room
- Tape a French sentence or phrase to the shower and memorise it for a week, then change it
- Greet your friends and family in French, even if they don't understand you or think you sound silly
- Talk to your dog or cat in French – they don't know what you're saying, anyway

Chapter 1 Review

Key points discussed in this chapter:

- Your reasons for learning French may vary, but the key is to keep yourself constantly motivated. Make your motivations as exciting, inspiring, and relevant as possible.
- When learning French, consider your personal passions or interests, make use of variety in your study methods and resources, and add loads of positive thinking. It helps to choose quality study time over quantity of time!
- Motivation can be difficult to cultivate over long periods of time. But immersion, the most painless way of learning a language, will help you achieve your goals faster.
- A good way to ensure success in learning French is to make learning a daily habit. Insert something French into your daily routine, then mix it up with short-term, high-intensity goals.
- The formula for learning French successfully is to keep yourself motivated and turn it into a daily habit.

Chapter 2 –
Myths About Learning
the French Language

*I*f you tell someone that you are learning French, you will most likely receive one of the following reactions: *But that's such a hard language! Isn't it too difficult? Wow, you must be really smart to learn French!*

The French language has a reputation for being difficult. The reality is, learning any new language is difficult. If it is not your native tongue, it is going to be hard. This perception is particularly true for native English speakers regarding learning French.

The difficulties that native English speakers face are greater than those faced by people who grow up in a bilingual country. People who grow up in various countries around Europe have the advantage of speaking a primary language from birth as well as being exposed to English in early primary school through mandatory education. For example, in Canada, both English and French are spoken and both languages are highly relevant educationally and geographically, so bilingualism is easy to achieve.

However, in countries such as the United States and Australia where there is no "official second language," learning another language is not a top priority. This is especially true when the rest of the world is more inclined to learn English. Combined with the perception of how difficult it is to learn a language such as French, these factors make native English speakers reluctant to take up a second language.

This explains why French has gained the reputation of being "too difficult" and is often cast aside by English speakers. The irony here is that, while learning French has its challenges, it actually is not quite as difficult as learning English.

What's Difficult about French?

There are many stumbling blocks that learners of French come across in the early stages of getting to know this language. From mispronouncing words to using the wrong gender article, these difficulties cause common mistakes to occur. The most important thing to remember is that these difficulties become easier with increased familiarity with the language. At first, the French language may seem like a maze of confusing details, but these areas can easily become clear with time and patience.

Pronunciation is a nightmare.

The way that French words are pronounced is a significant difficulty faced by people learning French. One of the first stumbling blocks that learners of French come across is the question, "Do I pronounce this consonant?" French words commonly have silent letters that are a pronunciation trap for non-native speakers.

There are some classic examples common to the non-French speaking world, such as:

Words ending in **X**: *Bordeaux, faux, roux*

Words ending in **T**: *cabernet, rapport, poulet*

Within French pronunciation, there are three categories of letters that are silent. These include:

Silent E	When the letter **E** appears with no accent, it is generally silent
Silent H	The letter **H** is always silent. One of the following also applies: *Muet,* meaning that the **H** is silent and contractions and liaisons are required, as if the word starts with a vowel (e.g.: l'homme) *Aspiré,* meaning it is not pronounced, but acts like a consonant so a contraction is not permitted (e.g.: la hache, le hockey)
Final consonant	Letters that are usually silent are: **D, G, M, N, P, S, T, X, Z** Letters that are usually pronounced are: **B, C, F, K, L, Q, R**

The use of these silent letters means that words in French are not phonetic, which creates another difficulty for those learning the language. As frustrating as this can be when learning French, over time you will develop a sense for correlating the way words look with how they sound.

When in doubt, pronounce a word phonetically and see how it sounds. It will probably sound awful. For example, the word for bread is *pain*. If you try to say that word phonetically in English, it will sound like you are about to have a painful sandwich. The vowel combination of 'ai' and the silent 'n' means the word is pronounced with a nasal 'pa'. Anyone learning French will come across these amusing phonetic pronunciations. You only need to hear a French word pronounced incorrectly once to know never to repeat it that way again.

The example of the word *pain* also highlights complicated vowel combinations. Vowels are difficult in any language, so this is not just a problem with French. What makes French vowels more difficult is that they have long and short sounds. Also, vowels are not diphthongs as they are in English. This means that the vowel sound is not followed by a 'y' or 'w' sound; rather, it remains constant.

The following table explains the general rule for French vowels:

Hard vowels	**A, O, U**	Consonants such as **C, G, S** have a hard sound when followed by these vowels
Soft vowels	**E, I**	Consonants such as **C, G, S** have a soft sound when followed by these vowels
Nasal Vowels	**A, E, I, O, U**	When followed by **M** or **N**, vowels usually have a nasal sound made by expelling air through the mouth and nose
Accents	**A, E, I, O, U**	Vowel sounds change when they have an accent. This will be explained in more detail in another section

Masculine and feminine words.

Another major difficulty when learning French is the fact that nouns and adjectives have a gender. This does not exist in English, where an inanimate object has the gender-neutral preposition label of 'the' or 'a'.

The knife = le couteau (masculine)
The fork = la fourchette (feminine)

For the most part, the gender of a word is easy to distinguish because of the article 'la' or 'le'. However, this becomes complicated with words that start with a vowel.

The bird = l'oiseau (masculine)
The water = l'eau (feminine)

Added to this difficulty is the letter H in French. When a word starts with an H, it takes on the quality of a vowel.

The grass = l'herbe (feminine)
The hotel = l'hôtel (masculine)

Many French learners are confused by these gender rules. While the words with the gender article 'la' or 'le' are not too hard, it can seem impossible to figure out what gender words starting with a vowel are meant to be.

Fortunately, there is a general rule for word endings in French at helps with this. This rule applies to nouns.

Masculine	Feminine
-age	-tion, -sion, -son
-ment	-ure
-il, -ail, -eil, -ueil	-ude, -ade
-eau, -ou	-ée, té
-isme	-ière
-er, -oir	-euse
-ing	-ance, -ence

Of course, there can be exceptions to this rule. However, after learning more French vocabulary, you begin to develop a feel for the words and it becomes easier to identity what is masculine and what is feminine.

Words with a gender do not stop there, however. Just as in English, prepositions change depending on context. The difficulty with French is that the preposition always has to agree with the gender of the word.

English	French Masculine	French Feminine
The	Le	La
My	Mon	Ma
Your	Ton	Ta

Consider the following sentence:

My father is very happy
Mon père est très heureux

The 'mon' and 'heureux' are both used because the sentence is referring to someone or something masculine, in this case a father. Everything changes, however, if the main focus of the sentence is someone or something feminine. For example:

My mother is very happy
Ma mère est très heureuse

This rule is easy enough to follow. When referring to a mother, it is clear that everything in the sentence needs to be feminine because the article is a female. Now, what happens when something can be *either* masculine *or* feminine? Consider, for example, a dog:

If you are talking about a male dog, a sentence will be:

The dog is cute
Le chien est mignon

But for a female dog, a sentence will be:

La chienne est mignonne

In instances like this, it is best to hope that the dog has an obvious name to let you know if it is a boy or girl so you know which gender to use.

The accents look funny and make funny sounds.

The French language is notorious for having a whole bunch of accents that can confuse the people learning it. The French alphabet has the same 26 letters as English, but glyphs added to the letters mix things up a bit. Compared to knowing English, a language without any accents, it can be quite daunting to look at words with symbols atop some of the letters. What many learners of French come to realize with time is that the accents actually make a lot of sense in terms of pronunciation.

The first thing to know about accents is that they only appear on vowels and the letter **C**. There are five types of accents to be aware of:

Grave (accent grave): ` this can be used on **A, E,** or **U** (Example: à la maison)

Acute (accent aïgu): ´ this can only be used on an **E** (Example: métier)

Circumflex (accent circonflexe): ^ this can be used on any vowel, **A, E, I, O, U**. A circumflex generally indicates in the English translation that an **S** is used to follow that vowel. (Example: *forêt = forest, hôpital = hospital*)

Diaresis (le tréma): ¨ this only appears on **E, I** or **U** and is used when two vowels are beside each other and both need to be pronounced. (Example: *naïve*)

Cedilla (une cédille): ¸ this can only be used on the letter **C**. Without the cedilla, the **C** is always a hard

C, like a **K** sound. With the cedilla, it softens to an **S** sound, as in *garçon*. A cedilla is never used when **C** is followed by **I** or **E** because these vowels automatically soften the **C**.

The word order is jumbled up compared to English.

Yet another difficulty that native English speakers face when learning French is the different word order and sentence structure. English and French share the basic subject-verb-object syntax when it comes to sentence formation. Differences appear, however, when sentences become more detailed and adjectives, articles, and negated verbs become involved.

Let's look at this sentence for an example:

Le petit chien blanc

A literal translation of the French sentence into English, following the same word order, would result in:

The little dog white

Instead of:

The little white dog

The subject of the dog is in a different place in the two sentences. In French, the adjectives come after the subject rather than before the subject, as they do in English.

It is not just the word order that makes things difficult with translations. Some French expressions translate differently into English. For example, to ask "How old are you?" in French, the phrase is "Quel âge avez-vous," which means *which age do you have?* Another common example is introducing yourself in French. In English, we say "My name is," but the French equivalent is "Je m'appelle" which means *I call myself.*

The perceived jumbling of the word order between English and French makes translation difficult. Sentences simply cannot be translated literally between the two languages. Understanding the syntax and grammar of the French sentence structure comes easily with time and patience.

French is spoken too quickly.

People learning French will often have initial difficulties with how fast the language is spoken. This is not a problem unique to the French language. Almost any foreign language sounds like it is spoken at a rapid rate for ears that are not accustomed to it. Think about how fast English must sound to a non-native speaker. Throw colloquial language into the conversation and of course all the words sound like they are rolling together.

English is a stress-timed language. This means that the length of syllables varies. French, on the other hand, is syllable-timed, which means that all syllables have the same length. English relies on pitch and intonation to make the sentence flow. Because of this, spoken English sentences can change from person to person, from accent to accent.

For example, an American English speaker might say the sentence: "This is good…"

If an Australian English speaker was to say the same sentence, the terminal inflection of this accent would cause it to sound unintentionally like a question: "This is good?"

Spoken French sentences, however, flow in a different manner. While the pitch and syllables of words stay the same in French, contractions and liaisons contribute to making it sound like a fast language.

Take this sentence in French, for example:

Les hommes mangent beaucoup d'abricots

First, the liaison between 'les' and 'hommes' makes it sound like one singular word. Secondly, the contraction with 'd'abricots' essentially takes two words and morphs them together in speech. To a non-native French ear, this makes it difficult to match the words to the sounds and, therefore, French sounds like a very fast paced language to listen to.

Where to start with the verb tenses?

From the imperfect to the subjunctive, verb tenses can feel like a total maze. Once again, this is not confusing just because it is in French. Verb tenses appear in every language and pose difficulties for all non-native speakers. A Japanese speaker learning Spanish would be just as confused with verb tenses as an English speaker learning French.

There are two main verb types that cause difficulties when learning French. These are the *verbe pronominal* and verbs with a preposition, such as *à* or *de*.

Verbe Pronominal

These are verbs that include reflexive actions and therefore need a reflexive pronoun to accompany them in addition to a subject pronoun. It is much more common in French than it is in English. In English, we would say, *"We are getting dressed."* The French equivalent to this is, *"We are dressing ourselves,"* and a reflexive verb is used: *"Nous nous habillons."*

Pronominal verbs can be used in three different ways:

- Reflexive verbs (a reflexive action)

- Reciprocal verbs (a reflexive action between two parties, for example: *s'adorer* = *to love one another*)

- Idiomatic pronominal verbs (a reflexive expression, for example: *se rendre* = *to go*).

Pronominal verbs are most commonly used in the reflexive form. This means that the subject of the verb is performing an action upon himself, herself, or itself. These mainly refer to parts of the body, clothing, or personal circumstances.

Reflexive verbs are just like normal verbs with a reflexive pronoun in the beginning.

Je me douche = I take a shower

Tu te lèves = you wake up

Verb prepositions

Prepositions are used in English as well as French to give a verb a certain meaning. They make verbs complete in a sentence, such as "to look at" or "to take care of"; prepositions are required. Prepositions are different for French and English words. The **most common** prepositions in French are *à* and *de*. They are used in the following instances:

à + infinitive
This is used when verbs and phrases are followed by an infinitive, such as *apprendre à parler le français = to learn how to speak French*.

à + indirect object
There is no English equivalent preposition for this, but this is used regarding an indirect object, such as *acheter à quelqu'un = to buy to someone*.

de + infinitive
This is used when verbs are followed by an infinitive, such as *choisir de* or *essayer de*.

de + indirect object
Once again, this is used when an indirect object follows a verb, such as *partir de* or *jouer de*.

The best way to memorize these prepositions is to practice. Reading is one of the best ways, in my opinion, to master the preposition. Do not worry if you make mistakes. We are looking to improve your French step by step. The preposition should not be your priority.

What's Not So Difficult About French?

You know the English alphabet; therefore you know the French one.

The English and French languages share a long history of influencing one another. This is why they share the same 26 letters of the alphabet. This makes French words easy to recognize for English speakers. Furthermore, the fundamental 26 letters are common amongst other languages, such as Italian and Spanish.

When it comes to French, the letters are easily recognizable for an English speaker. It is just the pronunciation that varies slightly. The most distinct changes between French and English sounds are:

H is silent in French

E is pronounced 'euh', as in *elephant*

I is pronounced 'ee', as in *Italy*

R is the French guttural R sound

French words are hidden in English.

The English language is sprinkled with French words. Sure, these words are often mispronounced and lack the French accent, but the spelling is there. The reason French and English are so intertwined goes back to the history of the two languages.

Chapter 2 – Myths About Learning the French Language

The Norman Conquest of England in 1066 has much to do with this. William the Conqueror became the King of England, and as such the French language became the primary language spoken in the court and the administration. Gradually, French replaced English as the dominant language.

During this period, over 10,000 French words were integrated into the English language. Many of these vocabulary words are still in use today, particularly relating to government, law, and literature. Beyond this, more than a third of all English words are derived from French. Some of the most common examples can be found when it comes to food. Just think about it the next time you order cuisine from the *à la carte* menu, such as the *soupe du jour* with a *baguette*.Be sure to say "Bon appétit" when the meal comes.

English has more exceptions to (grammar) rules than French.

Remember all of that stuff about gender and verbs and tenses in French? Remember how confusing all the rules, and all of the exceptions to the rules, are? Those things do make learning French difficult, certainly. But take another look at English. The English language is a minefield of rules and exceptions that make it much more difficult to learn than French.

Let's use this well-known English rule as an example:

I before E, except after C.

This is said to be "the supreme rule for English spelling."

Now, let's see how one sentence can break this rule:

Eight foreigners came to a sovereign land to visit their neighbours and climb a mountain of great height.

In fact, only 44 words in English actually follow this rule. There are 923 words that are an exception to the rule. So, while French may have its grammatical challenges and difficulties, always remember that your native language is not all that easy, either.

I am not here to teach you English, however, just to give you some perspective :)

French verb conjugations actually are not that scary.

French verb conjugations are the reason behind the most common difficulties learners of the language have. Verbs in English are just as difficult as they are in French. What is great about French verbs is that they are easier to categorize and they follow patterns, whereas English verbs can be more arbitrary and have more exceptions.

Let's focus on the present, past, and future tenses for this example of French verbs. There are three categories of infinitive verbs to look at. These are verbs that end in *er, ir* or *re.*

Type of verb	Infinitive (infinitif)	Present tense	Passé composé (auxiliary + verb)	Future (future)
er verbs – completely regular	Manger – to eat	Je mange	J'ai mangé	Je mangerai
ir verbs – mostly regular	Dormir – to sleep (irregular)	Je dors	J'ai dormi	Je dormirai
re verbs – mostly irregular	Prendre – to take (irregular)	Je prends	J'ai pris	Je prendrai

In the present tense with regular verbs, conjugations are simple. The first person, second person, third person singular and plural all sound the same when spoken – they are just spelled differently. For example:

Je mange

Tu manges

Il mange

Nous mangeons

Vous mangez

Ils mangent

While irregular verbs can seem intimidating, there are not too many of them. Most of them can be grouped into the same category. Most irregular verbs are very common, so they are easy to remember. *Faire* and *être* are good examples of irregular verbs. These are among the first verbs a learner of French comes to know well as they are used in all tenses very often.

At the end of this eBook, I will share a lot of verbs and resources to help you master the French verbs.

Chapter 2 Review

Myths Regarding Learning French

French has gained a reputation for being a hard language to learn. That should not necessarily be the case. Once you know what these French language learning myths are, it will be easy for you to grab it by the horns and tackle the issues once and for all.

As a recap of the chapter, here are the common learning difficulties and how to fix them:

- **French pronunciation.** This need not give you nightmares at all. Begin by having a good grasp of the general pronunciation rules, including the silent letters and the vowels, and slowly make your way from there.

- **Masculine and feminine words.** Word genders can be a huge pain for learners, but you can distinguish them easily with the help of the articles that come before each word. Arm yourself with knowledge of general rules and conquer this challenge once and for all.

- **Accents.** Accents - the look and sound of it - spell trouble for most. Instead of thinking of accents as the enemy, consider them your good friends who help you in distinguishing the proper pronunciation.

- **Word order and sentence structure.** French sentences can be perceived as big, jumbled messes by new learners. But at their foundations are a basic subject-verb-object syntax similar to English. As you progress to lengthier complex sentences, however, there will be differences in the order of the adjectives, negated verbs, and articles. The only remedy to this is time and patience. Given enough time, you will breeze through these too.

- **French is spoken too fast.** Not necessarily. It is basically the same with other languages, though French liaisons and contractions may make speaking sound like rapid fire. Practice listening to French and insert it into your daily routine. Soon, you will make sense of it quite easily.

Once you approach learning French with an open, positive frame of mind, you will be quick to realize the easy aspects. Bear in mind that it is not at all scary and you, (yes, you!) are quite ready to take the challenge. So, go for it!

Chapter 3 –
Myths about General Language
Learning

Immersion is all you need to learn a language

*I*mmersion is the process of being surrounded by the culture of the language you are learning. This is generally best done by living in or visiting a native-speaking country for a long period of time. Immersion is certainly an effective way to learn the language, particularly colloquial expressions and local sayings. However, it is naïve to believe that you can learn the language properly by simply being around it.

Without an understanding of the grammar and syntax of the language, the spoken words you are hearing have little context. This means that, although you are speaking on a daily basis, you may be speaking incorrectly. When you learn a language purely through immersion and listening, you are more likely to mispronounce a word, not understand the grammar order of the sentence, and have a smaller vocabulary.

For example, learning French through immersion means you will speak French all the time. But if you mishear the way something is said, this mistake can become ingrained in your manner of speaking. These types of mistakes can be little things, but they can make a big grammatical difference when written. An example of this in English is if someone says, "He made tea?" instead of asking the complete question, "Did he make tea?" These grammatical errors occur easily in spoken, colloquial conversation in any language.

This is also true for attempting to learn a language solely by speaking it. The practice of speaking French is highly important for developing fluency, speaking with confidence, and having an enhanced accent. However, it is still important to support the spoken elements of French with an understanding of all other aspects of the language. The practices of speaking and immersion are most effectively done with reading and writing simultaneously so that you understand the grammar and syntax of the language.

"I'm too old to learn a new language"

There is no denying that it becomes harder to learn a language the older you get. This, however, does not mean it is impossible. The acquisition of a first language is through immersion and lived experiences. Learning a second language needs to be done differently to account for the decreased neuroplasticity in the brain. Throughout primary school and early high school, it is still really easy to absorb a new language. As the brain develops and different cognitive processes take place, however, this becomes more challenging the older you get.

The biggest challenge one faces when learning a second language as an adult is finding an opportunity to learn. As children, the opportunity to learn a language is integrated into the school curriculum and all the resources are provided as part of a class. Adults, however, must be self-motivated and find the time to learn a language independently. This can obviously be hard when trying to find a balance between work life and family as well as making time to learn a new language.

When learning a language as an adult, always keep in mind that success is measured differently as you get older. Any time you dedicate to learning a new language is an achievement. Any progress you make is worth celebrating along the way. Pace yourself, take your time, and remember that you are keeping your brain active and healthy by learning a new language.

Learning a language is too expensive

To successfully learn French, you have to invest time and effort into the process, as well as some money. There are many online learning methods that claim to help you achieve fluency in French in just a few weeks. These are generally expensive software programs that use a crash-course intensity method to give you the basics of French. Unfortunately, these generally do not result in fluency.

Rather than short-term investments in learning French or any language, it is best to commit to a long-term process of immersing yourself in the language. Give yourself realistic expectations for learning the language, rather than doing a week-long intensive stint and expecting immediate results.

Here are some ways you can enhance your French studies without buying expensive software or taking a costly course:

- Buy a French language book and pick a word a day to learn the meaning and spelling of, and use it in a sentence. A good book to use as a learning tool is "Hugo in 3 months".

- Listen to French podcasts from the internet.

- Watch YouTube clips or French movies.

- Read interesting French blog posts or news articles.

- Use websites such as iTalkii or Livemocha to chat to other French learners and practice your written French.

- Whenever possible, have conversations using French. Speak as much as you can in French; sometimes you can do this by greeting your friends and family in French, even if they don't understand what you're saying.

"My foreign accent sounds terrible!"

When a French person speaks English, you can hear a distinct accent. But if a French person has been speaking English for 20 years and living in an English speaking country, the accent is only subtle. When you start off learning any new language, your accent will not be perfect.

There is no quick-fix solution to developing a native sounding accent. It takes time and practice to achieve this.

Pronunciation is probably the aspect of a language that requires the most practice among other skills. Pronunciation needs to come before in-depth knowledge and increasing your vocabulary in French, which can be frustrating. It can be easy to learn a new word and recognize it when written, but the word is useless if you cannot pronounce it or recognise how it is said. This is similar to learning to play basketball and being shown by a coach how to do a 3-point shot. You can see how it is meant to be done and how the end result should look, but it will take days or weeks before you are able to make a nice and elegant shot. The same is true with pronunciation; it will take time and many attempts to master how your tongue and lips need to move in order to correctly pronounce words in French.

Using some of the following study/practice methods below can assist you in losing the foreign sound to your French accent.

Study phonetics

The best way to understand pronunciation is to study the phonics of a language. This is difficult when learning French because it is not a phonetic language. However, you can gain a better understanding of how the letters sound by studying the alphabet and the sound the letters make on their own. Also pay attention to how an accent changes the sound of a letter and what sounds vowel combinations make together.

Listen to French

Listening is the best way to improve your speaking. Whether it is through conversation, radio, music, podcasts or movies, opening your ears to French will help you grasp how the language sounds. This will help you pick up colloquial language as well as become attuned to the pace, stress, and intonation of sentences and words.

Listen to yourself

Recording yourself speaking in French is one of the best ways to enhance your speaking abilities. Although it can be a little intimidating, it is a highly effective way to hear your mistakes as they occur. If you never listen to yourself speak, you will never know what you are doing right or wrong. It is much better to fix something early on so that mistakes do not become a habit.

Read out loud

Reading a written text aloud can give you a good feel for how French words sound. This also allows you to widen your vocabulary and see the sounds that letters make when placed together. Having the written material in front of you provides a good connection to the relationship between written and spoken French. You can also use this website to practice your pronunciation. Reading and listening to the native French speaker read the different stories will help you to master the pronunciation rules in French: http://www.languageguide.org/french/readings/

*Pronunciation – the letter **R***

The letter **R** is universally difficult in just about any language. The guttural **R** in French can make it difficult to get achieve fluent-sounding accent. The **R** either rolls off the tongue or it is a guttural sound and comes from the throat. The only way to achieve a perfect **R** is to practice, practice, and practice some more.

English is the universal language, so why learn anything else?

If you are a native English speaker, you can certainly consider yourself lucky. English is an extremely useful language and most countries aspire to learn it as their second language. This is for education and business purposes. Speaking English gives you a number of worldwide travel and employment opportunities.

It may be a shock, then, to realize that only 5% of the world's population actually speaks English. The other 95% speaks another language. Sure, that 95% are probably learning English as their second language. This means that English is enough to 'get by' around the world. But by only speaking English when you travel to other countries, you will miss many things.

By speaking another language, you gain the following invaluable skills:

Improved memory

By learning a second language, you train your mind to remember additional details. This also has long-term benefits for helping to prevent Alzheimer's disease by keeping the brain active. While it can seem too challenging at first to remember all the finer details of learning a second language, you may just surprise yourself by how quickly you pick everything up and are able to recall the new grammar and vocabulary you have learned.

Cultural perspective

When you take on a second language, you learn much more than just a few new words and phrases. You also learn about an entirely new culture. Whether it is French, Japanese, or Spanish, you gain insights into the culture of the countries where the language is spoken. You learn about the history, lifestyle, literature, sports, and food as you study a language which fills your world with new ways of thinking and appreciating these things.

Improved English or native language

Grammar and syntax are a huge part of learning a second language. As you begin to understand these aspects of language, you begin to pay more attention to them in your native language. The translation process helps with this understanding and brings certain things about your native language to your attention that you may have overlooked previously.

Better job prospects

Speaking another language looks great on your resume or CV. It is a highly valuable skill in all areas of work. Whether you are working in a corporate business, as a teacher, or as nurse or doctor, there will always be an opportunity to use a second language. This can make you highly employable and help you get the job over a competitor.

Ability to travel with more than an online translator

If you are travelling to other countries where English is not the first language, you can probably survive with their broken English and the use of an online translator. But this process means having the translator tool, app, or bulky dictionary readily available and stumbling through pronunciations of the phrases you need. Speaking the language allow for a much more authentic interaction with the local culture and will be greatly rewarding if you put in the effort.

Chapter 3 Review

Myths and Truths About Language Learning

Pre-conceived ideas can often be a hindrance to learning a new language. Do not let these notions worry you. Chapter 3 delved into details of different myths about language-learning. Here is a quick recap:

- *Immersion is all you need to learn a language* (MYTH): Immersion helps, but it has to be done simultaneously with writing and reading in order to effectively understand correct grammar and syntax.

- *"I'm too old to learn a new language"* (MYTH): No one is too old to learn a new language. It is more challenging due to certain factors, but it is far from impossible.

- *Learning a new language is too expensive* (MYTH): It does not need to be very costly. However, you do have to invest time, effort and, yes, a bit of money, into the process.

- *"My foreign accent sounds terrible!"* (MYTH): While this may be true at the start, you can always keep practicing until you acquire an acceptable accent. There are several practice methods you can make use of.

- *"English is the universal language, why learn anything else?"* (MYTH): By learning a new language, you open yourself up to new opportunities and gain access to valuable skills.

Chapter 4 –
Study Methods: How to Improve your Listening

*B*eing able to listen to French and understand the spoken aspect of the language is highly important. This enables you to have confidence when listening to native French speakers. It can be very intimidating at first because French sounds incredibly fast paced and foreign to an untrained ear.

The ability to listen to spoken French fluently certainly comes before being able to speak it. Many French learners are frustrated by their inability to speak the language as well as they want to. A common cause of this is that listening skills are not developed enough. Listening is the fundamental skill in language-learning and once this is mastered, speaking and other elements of French come easily. The main advantage of practicing your listening skills in French is that it is an easy aspect to organize. Listening can be done actively or as part of the background noise in your life. Listening can be done through a range of resources and can be enjoyable and comfortable. The more you are exposed to French and the more you listen to it, the more attuned your brain will become to hearing spoken French.

This chapter will introduce you to some things you can do throughout your French studies to go from hearing jibber-jabber when someone speaks French to understanding each word that is said.

Focus on Pronunciation

The first step in listening to French is having an understanding of how French should sound. Pronunciation is the key to this. French is not a phonetic language, so pronunciation can be challenging since the written words often look much different than how they sound when spoken.

When you start out learning French, focus on pronunciation in the following ways:

o Learn the alphabet and how each letter sounds individually

o Concentrate on the vowel sounds, how they sound on their own, and how this changes when two vowels are placed together in a word (i.e., *au*)

o Listen to the sound consonants make when they are placed together (i.e., *sh, th*)

o Take a closer look at accents and how these change the sound of the letter (i.e., *à* vs *á*)

o Keep in mind liaisons between words that start with a vowel and how these change the sound of words

o Keep an ear out for the nasal sound on some letters. This generally occurs when a vowel is followed by an *m* or *n*

o Be mindful of the letter *h* as this is silent, either *aspiré* or *muet*

Once you have a basic understanding of French pronunciation, you can put it into practice by doing a range of listening activities.

Start out Small

Listening activities are challenging, sometimes even in your native language. It can be tempting when learning French to watch a French movie and tell yourself that you are learning listening skills through this. It is a valid thought, but it is important to first start small with listening tasks. A movie is long and has fast, conversational dialogue. In the early days of learning French, you are likely to get lost and confused throughout the movie, especially if you attempt to watch it without subtitles.

For this reason, it is better to start with a small listening task. Once you have mastered the skill of listening to and fully comprehending short recordings intended for beginners, then you can progress to listening to YouTube clips and eventually watching movies. If you start out expecting to understand a full movie, your confidence lessened and motivation to move forward will lessen.

After a few beginners' recordings, move up to intermediate recordings with more challenging vocabulary. Audio books are another great way to listen to French as they tell an interesting, continual story. These are generally available in beginner, intermediate, and advanced levels.

When listening to anything in French, always remember that there are probably words you will not understand. Do not panic when this happens. Keep listening, rather than pausing it, and see if you can infer from the context of the rest of the sentence what was being said. If necessary, listen to the sentence two or three more times and you will pick up what was said. This is an excellent listening comprehension improvement method.

Use the Right Resource

Depending on what level your French is up to, you need to pick a suitable audio tool to support your learning process. There is no point choosing an expert-level recording when you are a beginner at French, and vice versa.

Once you have an appropriate level recording, use the following sequence to practice your listening:

1. Listen to the sentence a few times.

2. If you do not understand the first few times, take it back to the start and listen again.

3. For words you do not understand, write them down phonetically. Repeat the recording and see if you understand the word. If you do not understand it after a few times, look it up and make note of it. This is a great way to build your vocabulary.

4. Do the above step for all words you do not understand. After this, go back and listen to the whole recording again. Do you understand it all now?

5. If you do not, listen to the translation to comprehend it better.

By taking these steps with recordings, you will find that your listening comprehension improves. As you progress through different levels and stages of French, these steps will become easier. Eventually, most steps will become unnecessary and you will be able to understand fluently the first time.

Active Listening

When you are listening to anything in French, at any stage of your studies, it is important to practice active listening. This is the opposite of passive listening, which is listening to something in the background, such as a song. Passive listening can be useful to reinforce things you already know and the French you have already studied. When you listen to something actively, your brain tunes in and absorbs the information better. Active listening can be done in a number of different ways, including some of the following methods.

Listen and Repeat

Chapter 4 – Study Methods: How to Improve your Listening

While listening to a recording in French, whether you are a beginner or at a higher level, pause the recording and repeat what was said. It does not matter if you do not remember it word for word; it is just important to try and repeat the general gist of the sentence to improve your comprehension.

Listen and write (aka dictation)

When listening to a recording, have a notepad beside you and try to write down what is being said in French. This is excellent for your listening comprehension and vocabulary skills. At the beginning stages, start small and work with just one sentence at a time, pause, and write it down. As you progress, try working with paragraphs while doing this. Once you have written out a fair amount of the recording, listen to it again and read your writing as you go. This will give you a chance to see what parts of the recording you dictated correctly and where mistakes were made.

On the Talk in French website, 10 such dictations are available for free. Check them out here.

Listen and Read

Audio books and recordings with a transcript are a fantastic way to read and listen simultaneously. As the audio is playing, read along the pages and see the relationship between spoken and written French.

Listen to Yourself

It may seem intimidating to record yourself speaking French, especially during the beginning stages of learning the language. However, this is a highly important study skill to have. By recording yourself and listening to yourself speak French, you will hear the words you mispronounce, which will help you develop a better accent. After a few times of doing this, your confidence will improve and you will be more aware of what sounds you need to make to perfect your French accent.

Build Yourself up to Conversational French

Even when you are just beginning to learn French, try to keep in mind that the ultimate outcome you are hoping for is to be able to listen to conversational French and understand it. Listening to conversational French is quite different than listening to recordings and books as it is colloquial and authentic.

Recordings and audio books aim to consist of clearly spoken sentences that are grammatically correct. However, think about how you speak conversationally in your native tongue. It is, more often than not, grammatically incorrect – sentences are shortened and words are blended together. This is the same for conversational French.

To prepare yourself for conversational French, it is highly important that you take all of the aforementioned steps into consideration when practicing your listening with correct study skills. Once you have a solid understanding of French pronunciation, grammatical sentence structure, and have listened to a wide range of resources at different stages of the learning process, you will have much more confidence when listening to conversational and colloquial French. Some ways that you can do this include:

o **Listening to the news or watching TV.** This will give you exposure to clear, concise sentences that contain information presented at a reasonable pace. There are many websites to stream French news and television, such as the one here.

o **Listening to music.** Here, you will hear spoken French in a different tone and with nuanced conversation. This will help attune your ear to hearing familiar words vocalised at a different volume or pace.

o **Listening to the radio.** French radio gives you a good chance to practise listening without any visual cues. French radio can be streamed online at websites such as RFI.

o **Listening to podcasts.** Here, spoken French can be informative or humorous, depending on the type of podcast. Whenever possible, try to listen to a podcast with two people speaking so that you hear French spoken back and forth.

o **Watching YouTube clips.** These are great because they are generally short so you do not have to focus for too long. There are plenty of funny French videos, recordings by comedians, or silly French commercials that can give you a good laugh while improving your listening comprehension. Even better, YouTube clips are free and easily accessible. Here (https://www.youtube.com/user/GoldenMoustacheVideo) are some amusing French YouTube clips to get you started.

o **Watching movies.** French spoken in movies is conversational dialogue, generally between two or more people. At first, watch with subtitles so that you get a feel for the pace of the language and have something to refer to if you do not understand at first. As you improve, remove the subtitles and see how well your ear can pick up the conversation. Movies are a great resource as they have motion pictures to give you context to what is being spoken. Again, I shared a list of French movies to watch on my website. Here is an example: http://www.talkinfrench.com/28-days-french-movie/

o **Listening to native conversational French.** If you are lucky enough to go to a French speaking country, take a day or two to just listen to what is being said around you. Keep in mind that French can sound different depending on the accent or region you are in, such as the differences between Canadian French, African French, and European French.

Create a Habit

Once listening to French becomes a habit in your life, you will begin to feel odd if you do not hear any French at some point in your day. Creating a habit of listening to a little bit of French each day is a fantastic learning strategy that will continuously expose your ears to the French language.

Making a habit of listening to French can start on day one of your French studies. Here are some tips on how you can incorporate French as a habit in your life:

o Have an app on your phone, such as Babbel or Duolingo, to practice a small listening exercise each day.

o Make the most of your time, such as your daily commute to work or lunch break, to listen to a French podcast or audiobook.

o Create a French playlist of songs to listen to at the gym or when you go for a walk or run. I have a Spotify playlist you can check out on my website. It is free and legal. http://www.talkinfrench.com/french-music/ (you can also try the service deezer).

o Listen to something in French while cooking dinner. Listening to French radio like France Culture can be great.

o Listen to French as you fall asleep so that your brain subconsciously absorbs the language.

Making French a habit in your life is an essential part of training your brain to recognise French sounds. This will help greatly when it comes to listening to native conversational French. By listening to a little bit of French each day, it will be less of shock for your brain to switch over to hearing French words and fully comprehending what is being said.

While you still need to study the grammar and syntax of French sentences and pronunciation of French words, listening habits that you create will complement your studies. More tips on how to turn listening to French into a habit can be found here. Your listening habit can even be a reward for your French studies – save something that you enjoy listening to, like a favourite song or funny YouTube clip, and give your brain a treat after some hard core studying.

Chapter 4 Review

At this point, we have already established that learning a new language - and being fluent in it - can be quite tricky. So it pays if you have a few tricks up your sleeve, too. With an open mind, a strong desire to learn, and the right approach to learning, you should do quite well in a short time span.

To drive home all of the points discussed in this chapter, here is a small list of tips and practice tasks grouped into Do's and Don'ts.

First, the Don'ts:

- **Don't be lazy!** No matter how smart you are or how quickly you grasp ideas, you still need to make an effort each day to practice listening.

- **Don't think of your listening tasks as a huge burden.** You will learn so much faster if you are having fun.

- **Don't create long lists of items for memorization**. For now, focus on listening.

Now, the Do's:

- **Do try to learn like a baby.** Consider how babies first learn a language: imitating what they hear, repeating it over and over, not being self-conscious of errors, and eventually recognizing what words mean.

- **Do begin learning the pronunciation before anything else.** Understand the sounds first and naturally progress from there.

- **Do spend a huge chunk of your free time listening to French being spoken.** Each time you come across something you do not understand, write it down and research it later.

- **Do listen to French radio stations.** You can stream them from the internet. A good option is from RFI (journal Français Facile); there is a script that goes with it.

- **Do watch French movies.** Choose films that have English subtitles. The non-verbal cues will help you understand better what is happening, while the emotions the movie evokes will make you remember the dialogue better.

- **Do listen to French music.** There are plenty of wonderful French musicians to choose from. Listening to music will help you retain the French words in the lyrics. Learn the words and, later on, find out what they mean.

- **Do watch French videos on YouTube.**

- **Do make your own recording of French words and listen to it on repeat**.

- **Do find time to talk to native French speakers.** You can do this online or face-to-face.

Remember to choose the right resources as you go through all of these steps. When you are still starting out, choose beginner-level audio material. Skipping to the intermediate and advanced levels will only frustrate and discourage you.. Head over to talkinfrench.com for a list of recommendations and resources fit for each level.

Chapter 5 –
Study Methods: Get the Most
Out of Reading French

*T*he skill of reading French is incredibly useful in everyday life, whether you are learning French for work, travel, or pleasure. Being able to recognize words by sight makes life much easier, such as being able to glance at a French word in your study text book and understand it, to being in a French speaking country and being able to read a menu at a restaurant without any problems. Reading French can be enjoyable and engaging when you approach it with the right attitude. Some of the following tips can help you to make the most of reading and improving your reading skills.

Read with translations

Reading in a foreign language is undoubtedly an ambitious task. To avoid being overwhelmed at first by opening up a book and seeing pages filled with French words, start out by reading with translations.

Bilingual books

As you start out learning French, reading bilingual texts can be very useful. There are many books that have French on one page and a translation on the other page. The advantage to having the translation available is to support your comprehension. If there is a word or phrase you do not understand, you can refer to the translation. It is always important to remember that French often does not translate directly into English, so do not read the translation word for word.

Read something familiar

Another clever way to improve your reading with translations is to read something you already know well, but in French. Many popular books have French translations, such as the Harry Potter series. When you read content you are already familiar with, you already know what is happening in the story, so you can concentrate better on reading the French.

Find easy ways to translate

Translation can be a tedious process if the text you are reading is not bilingual. Having to open your dictionary for every second word can be off-putting and take the enjoyment out of reading French. Fortunately, thanks to technology, a number of online translation services and dictionaries are available to make this easier. If you are reading a text online, there are many tools available to add to your web browser as an extension and allow you to translate a word at the click of a button.

As you progress with learning French, you will find that you need the translation less and less. Over time, you will go from needing the translation for most of the sentences to just a few words, and eventually just for clarify your understanding.

If you have an e-reader, like a Kindle, you can use a dictionary directly inside the device. Go to this link to learn how to do it: http://learnoutlive.com/how-to-use-your-kindle-to-study-a-foreign-language/

Read a Range of Resources

The wonderful thing about reading is that it comes in many different forms. Thanks to the internet, you have a plethora of reading resources at your disposal at the click of a button. This means that there is something available to suit all reading interests.

o **Newspaper:** there is a wide range of websites where you can access the French news. Reading the news in French not only helps with your reading skills, but also keeps you up to date with French society, such as what is happening in politics and culture. This is a useful way to become further immersed in French and motivate you to keep learning the language. Some websites include:

- *For beginning learners –* www.20minutes.fr and www.metro.fr, http://www.monquotidien.fr/
- *For intermediate learners –* www.leparisien.com
- *For advanced learners* – lemonde/lefigaro/ liberation

o **Books:** A number of French books can be purchased for online reading through Kindle, which provides you access to an endless range of reading material. If you prefer to read books on paper, it is always worth checking out second hand bookshops to see if there are any French language fiction or non-fiction books. Alternatively, these can be bought online as well. I recommend the following books: Lullaby (Le Clezio), Ibrahim et les fleurs du coran (Schmidt), La petite fille de Madame Linh (Claudel), L'étranger (Camus), and Ni d'ève ni d'adam (Nothomb).

o **Blog posts:** French language blogs are ideal because they are short, engaging, and cover a variety of topics. Blogs are not as formal as the news; they are generally written in first-person perspective and consist of personal accounts of the author's life and interesting things or she is doing around the world. The content is usually light and enjoyable to read. Some useful blogs can be found on the following websites:

- http://onethinginafrenchday.podbean.com/
- http://tour-du-monde-autostop.fr/
- http://www.blog-unfrancaisalondres.com/

- **Online articles:** Unlike the news, online articles such as those found on Buzzfeed tend to be funny and light-hearted. These can be great to read when you have just a little bit of free time, such as when you are taking a train or bus, or while your dinner is cooking. Some fun online articles can be found on these websites: http://www.buzzfeed.com/?country=fr

  - http://www.demotivateur.fr/

Take Notes As You Read

When you read, you are actively absorbing more than just information from the text you are studying. You are also being exposed to more French vocabulary, new ways sentences and phrases can be written, new verb conjugations, and other grammatical rules. All of this informs your French knowledge and increases your skill set. However, it can be overwhelming to remember everything as you read more and more texts.

Taking notes as you read a French document, article, or book is a great way to track the things you need to practice. For example, if you find you are making a lot of notes when verbs are conjugated, or when adjectives are used, this shows you that you need to pay attention to these areas of learning French.

Taking notes can be done in many different ways, depending on the type of text you are reading. Using sticky notes is a handy note-taking solution as you can write on the sticky note and mark the page as you go. Highlighting or underlining words is another good idea so that you know the exact word or sentence that was causing you difficulty.

Note taking is not just for focusing on the things you need to improve. You can also take notes when you find some interesting information and want to learn more about a topic.

Build Your Vocabulary

The most practical way to improve your reading is to improve your French vocabulary. If you think of your French skills as a tower, your vocabulary is the foundation of it. The sturdier the foundation, the better your reading, writing, speaking and listening skills, the building blocks of your tower, will be. The more French words you can recognize by sight, the more fluent your reading will become. There are many activities you can do to increase your vocabulary.

For example, learn a new word each day by making use of a French vocabulary list online or through apps on your phone. This is a more effective method of learning new vocabulary than using a paper dictionary, which can make finding new words an awkward process. For example, this website (http://www.transparent.com/word-of-the-day/today/french.html) provides a new French word each day. On the website you can see the word written, hear the audio, and see it used in a sentence.

Other websites such as these, http://ielanguages.com/french.html and http://www.digitaldialects.com/French.htm, have activities to build your vocabulary through fun games aimed at beginners and intermediate learners. This can be a light-hearted way to complement your French studies and reinforce some skills you already have.

There are also many apps available on Apple and Android devices that allow you to build your vocabulary through activities. Some apps for learning French include Memrise, SpeakEasy, Duolingo and FluentU.

Another helpful activity is to use vocabulary flash cards. Pick up a card and read the word aloud. Write it down and think of a sentence using the word. Doing these small activities on a daily basis will enhance your French vocabulary and allow you to understand better as you read anything new in French.

Learn Vocabulary With Context

Learning vocabulary words is important for reading, but these words need to have a context to make them relevant. For instance, if you learn the word *flower,* that is good. But what about more information on the flower? What colour is it? Where does it grow? Is it inside or outside?

Giving words context and an explanation helps with sentence building. This is not only a way to extend your vocabulary, but it also assists with reading as you become more familiar with sentence structure and have wider exposure to the elements that make up a sentence, such as prepositions, adjectives, and word order.

When you learn new words in French, another easy way to remember them is to relate the word to your own life. This type of word association causes you to think of a real life scenario in which that word has come in handy in your own life. This is particularly relevant when learning words related to food or shopping. For example, the word for *supermarket* can be easily memorized if each time you need to buy groceries, you remind yourself you need to go to the *supermarché.*

Read With Audio

Combining your visual learning skills with your listening skills will enhance your French on many different levels. If you have access to an audio book or a written transcript of a recording, listen and read at the same time. This will help you see the relationship between written and spoken French and pick up little nuances in how the language sounds compared to how it is written.

There are apps and websites available for immediate audio repetition of what you are reading. Some of these include www.lingq. com and www.bliubliu.com/en/. These are handy websites because they allow you to read and have the option to listen; they also feature some vocabulary building activities for unfamiliar words.

Read With Images

Visual learning is an invaluable way to enhance your reading skills and vocabulary building. When you learn new words or sentences, it is a good idea to have a pictorial representation of the word. This is why vocabulary flash cards often come with an image. When you begin learning French, seeing a picture of the word will help with memory association; for example, when you see the word *chat* and a picture of a cat, you will remember the word more easily.

Some ways that you can enhance your learning with visual aids include:

- Creating your own picture dictionary, if you like drawing. Each time you learn a new word, write it down in a notebook and draw an image beside it.

- Downloading an app to your phone, such as Babbel, or one that has flash cards embedded into the learning process.

- Buying a pack of vocabulary flash cards with images on them and review them daily.

- Checking out websites such as Memrise that assist with memorizing language vocabulary through the use of images.

- Labelling items around your home with the French word so that when you see them, you also see the French word. This helps you to think in French, as well as engaging your visual and kinaesthetic learning abilities by seeing and touching the items.

Read What You Enjoy

It is highly important that you enjoy what you are reading. If you have no interest in understanding the rules of golf, reading a manual all about golf will be a struggle. If you force yourself to read something in French that you do not understand, you will not be gaining anything out of the text. Sure, you might learn a few new words about a new topic, but you will not be engaged with the text.

When you are engaged and learning actively, your brain absorbs much more and you enjoy the learning process that much more. So if you are passionate about animals, read an article or book in French about your favourite animals. If you love sports, find a biography of your favourite sports player in French.

Similarly, it is also beneficial to read something you are familiar with. If you read the daily news in English and an article sparks your interest, try finding a French version or translation of the same report. This can be easily done over the internet. When you read the French equivalent of something you already know about, it will be much easier to comprehend the gist of the article and, therefore, you will spend less time trying to decipher what the article is about, and more time reading French.

Review What You Read

Repetition is the key to success when learning a new language. If you read a sentence and do not understand it, read it again. If you understand it the next time, read it again and memorize it. The more times you re-read something, the more vocabulary you will remember and the better you will become at recognizing different sentence structures and word order. This is why it is important to read material you enjoy, so you will be happy to go back and re-read it. If you find an article you thought was really funny, insightful, or motivational, keep it saved on your computer or bookmark it so you can refer back to it in a week's time.

o   Start with books written for children – these have sim-plified grammar and are stress free, plus they are fun and cute

o   Read French texts with translations so that you can see the word order and grammar variations, and can have a better understanding of the context of expres-sions and phrases

o   Read articles on what interests you – do not force your-self to read a topic that you find boring as this will not engage you or help with developing your reading com-prehension

o   Highlight or mark words that you do not understand as you read – try not to look them up immediately as this can interrupt the flow of reading. Rather, mark them and keep reading, as you might be able to decipher the meaning from the context of the rest of the sentence. If you still cannot, you can look up the word at the end of the chapter/paragraph

o

o   Look up a new French word each day in the dictionary – write it down, read it aloud, and use it in a sentence as a vocabulary building activity to enhance your read-ing skills

o   Study French with audio – read an article and listen to the transcript at the same time to see the relationship between written and spoken French.

Chapter 5 Review

This chapter discussed the many ways you can make use of reading to further your study of the French language. There is, however, one detail we should not neglect:

How does one learn to enjoy reading and pick it up as a hobby?

Needless to say, reading can be considered by many as an arduous task, something that seems like a lot of work. When you think of it this way, it could definitely hamper your learning progress, since we have established early on that to make something stick, you have to enjoy it and have fun doing it.

So the question is, *how do you make reading fun?*

Below are some tips on how to cultivate reading as a pleasurable experience:

- ☐ **Have a desire to read**. If you cannot find it in you, try motivating yourself. Think of how much more articulate you will become once you have developed a reading habit. Think of how much depth it is going to add to your character. Reading opens up vast worlds you cannot even fathom. Reading is a way to exercise your mind and become an even better version of yourself.

- ☐ **Do not pressure yourself**. Reading should be fun. The moment it starts to stress you out, let go of what you are reading and start again.

- ☐ **Find the genre that appeals to you.** There is always a genre suited for everyone. Focus on your passions and interests and pick up a book, magazine, article or graphic novel that talks about it.

- ☐ **Always carry a book around.** Rather than force your-self to set a daily schedule which might make read-ing seem like work, bring a book with you everywhere you go or save an eBook in your smartphone or tablet. During your free time (e.g. while waiting for your next appointment, or in a long line to get your coffee, etc.), take out that book and start reading. If you choose the right book for you, reading snippets will make you look forward to reading more.

- ☐ **Schedule a special "book time" once a week.** Put effort into making it as special as possible. Choose some ambient music, light a candle, get your favourite munchies and then curl up on a comfy couch. If you are not the home-body type and are more outdoorsy, go out to your favourite spot, be it a park, the beach, or wherever, and have a cosy little picnic with your book.

- ☐ **Make a list of all the books you want to read.** On-line sites like Goodreads.com provide you with recom-mendations for books based on your chosen genre or author. List it down and work your way through your list. Make your list as interesting as possible to create a feeling of anticipation for the next book you will read.

- ☐ **Talk to readers.** Ask your reader friends for recommen-dations. They will be very happy to share insights and tips with you. It will amp up your desire to read further.

Reading is definitely one of the building blocks to learning and mastering a language. It also has numerous other benefits. So, go on, start cultivating a reading habit now. Your future self would thank you for it. And so will your French studies.

Chapter 6 –
Study Methods:
Top Ways to Speak French Better

Speaking is often perceived as one of the most challenging parts of learning French. This is because it takes confidence to speak another language while simultaneously concentrating on the grammatical structure and proper pronunciation of what you are saying. It may seem like a minefield of things to concentrate on, but there are small steps you can take during your studies of French to break down the stresses of speaking.

Listen to yourself speak

It seems obvious to say, but when you speak French you really need to *hear* yourself speak it. By paying attention to the way the words sound when you speak them, you will hear the slight nuances in your tone and gain a better understanding of how you need to control these in order to pronounce French words correctly.

As you focus on the sounds you are making, you also become more aware of how your mouth and tongue need to be positioned in order to articulate French words. A good way to do this in the beginning is to focus intently on phonics and the individual sound each letter makes.

As you progress with French and begin speaking full sentences, start recording yourself so that you can listen back to how you sound. Doing this will enable you to hear your French objectively. You will also be able to pick up on the sounds or words that you find challenging and correct yourself. After a few weeks of recording yourself and listening back to it, you will notice a drastic improvement in the way your French sounds. This is a great way to monitor your development with French.

Practise Commonly Used Phrases

There are certain French words and phrases that you will say more than others. These are the phrases that are important to focus on at the start of your French studies. Once you have nailed a few key phrases, your confidence will continually grow when speaking these and adding to them.

Some commonly used phrases you can practice and perfect the pronunciation of include:

- Hello/hi – *bonjour/salut*
- Goodbye/bye – *au revoir/à bientôt*
- How are you? – *comment allez-vous?*
- Thank you (very much) – *merci (beaucoup)*
- My name is – *je m'appelle*
- How much is… - *combien…*
- Where is... – *où est…*
- I'm sorry – *je suis désolé(e)*
- Do you speak English – *parlez vous anglais?*
- What time is it? – *quelle heure est-il?*

Buying a phrasebook can be a great and quick way for you to improve your French. Most phrasebooks (including the My Phrasebook eBook) have phonetics (e.g., s'il vous plait - seel voo pleh) specially created for tourists. I do not recommend using the phonetics part because it will not help you to pronounce French correctly; instead, just use the French phrases and listen to the MP3.

Converse any chance you get

Obviously, the best practice you can get with your French is talking to a native French speaker, or someone who is fluent. Sometimes, however, this is not always possible. Therefore, you should try to take any opportunity you get to practice speaking French.

Use basic phrases daily

You can practice speaking French by inserting some of the commonly used phrases mentioned above into your everyday life. Try greeting your friends, family, or co-workers in French. Even if they do not understand what you are saying, you can always clarify what you said after you have spoken. This way, you still get to practice French and perhaps even encourage other people in your life to learn a bit of it, too.

Converse online

There are other ways to have a proper conversation with French speakers or learners through the internet. Websites such as iTalki allow you to converse online. If you meet people during your travels or around your home city who are French, fluent in French, or are learning the language like you, exchange contact information and make the most of having a contact to converse with. Network-building is a fantastic way to keep up your French skills and gain confidence in speaking the language.

Talk to yourself

You can also try having a conversation with yourself, as crazy as it sounds. Speaking French while looking in the mirror allows you to see how your mouth moves around the words, which helps you form the sounds and pronunciations required for fluent French. Having a question and answer dialogue in the mirror gives you a chance to practice your French and also improve your confidence with the language.

Alternatively, why not talk to your pet cat or dog in French? They probably will not understand what you are saying anyway, but it can be a fun way to practice your French and make your pets bilingual at the same time.

Read out Loud

This is an invaluable skill that will enhance the way you speak, and understand, the French language. When you read aloud, you learn to articulate words and recognize the sound patterns the letters make. Since French is generally not a phonetic language, it can be difficult at first. Reading aloud is an effective way to compare how French words are written with how they sound, as there can often be quite a disparity between the two.

Remember, you do not have to read enormous chunks of French out loud. Just reading small sentences or phrases can really help with your speaking development. It is always best to start small so that you do not feel overwhelmed. If you concentrate on just a small section, you are less likely to make mistakes and have a better chance at improvement.

How to read aloud each day

o Read to someone else learning French, or a friend who is willing to listen even if they do not understand French.

o Post some French sentences and phrases on the outside of your shower door, and read them aloud while showering.

o Read a paragraph or two from a French book or article aloud each night before you fall asleep.

o Find some French recipes and read the ingredients and methods out loud while cooking.

o Label items around your home using sentences, such as *I want to eat bread (je voudrais manger le pain)* on the place where you store bread and say the sentence aloud each time you reach for the bread.

Turn these things into a habit

Creating a habit of speaking French each day is a really effective way to become immersed in the language. This is a good way to complement your studies of French. Take the following five steps into account in order to create a habit of speaking French aloud each day.

1. **Create a cue to encourage you to speak French aloud.** A cue can be something as basic as switching on the kettle for your morning cup of tea, or sitting down after dinner to watch some TV. Taking these small actions that are already part of your daily routine and using them as cues to speak French means the habit creation requires less effort on your part. It is just a matter of finding what works best for you in your daily schedule and when you feel most comfortable practicing speaking French aloud.

2. **Embed this cue into your routine.** This is where it is important to use a cue that is something you do daily, rather than something you do not do on a daily basis. For example, brushing your teeth before bed is done on a daily basis. This action can become a cue to speak something in French. You might have some French phrases stuck on the mirror and speak a different one each day, or have an app on your phone available after you are done brushing your teeth to help you practice speaking French aloud.

3. **Make the cue intentionally easy.** The idea of creating a habit is something so easy that it becomes effortless. There are certain things that you do each day that are just basic and easy, so much so that you find it more difficult to not do that task, such as checking the time when you know you need to be somewhere. When your cue to say something aloud in French is a simple task that you do anyway, it will become second nature to speak French.

67

4. **Ensure the cue is an easy action that you must undertake.** Learning French can be tiresome and exhausting if you are forcing yourself to sit down each day after work, open your books, and study long into the night. The idea of having a cue, such as brushing your teeth, to trigger this tedious action that you will not enjoy, is redundant. Rather, use the cue of brushing your teeth to do a simpler action, even something as basic as opening a French speaking app on your phone. When the action seems effortless, you are more inclined to do it. This is a way of tricking yourself into completing some of your French studying and speaking aloud, while feeling like all you are really doing is opening an app.

5. **Reward yourself after successfully doing this each day at the end of the week.** Rewards reinforce the positive behaviours you are doing while learning a language. At the end of the week, if you have successfully spoken a decent amount of French each day throughout your daily routine, you deserve to reward yourself. It can be anything from having a chocolate bar to getting a massage over the weekend. Whatever your reward is, do not hesitate to congratulate yourself on your language learning success, in French, and out loud. *Bon travail.*

Start thinking in French

If your internal dialogue is in French, it will be much easier for your spoken words to feel natural in French. The more you practice small phrases in French and the more you integrate speaking French as a habit into your everyday life, the more you will begin thinking in French.

Over time, as your French studies progress, you will notice that you begin needing internal translations less and less. For example, when you see a car, your first thought is to say the word 'car' in English. As you begin learning French, you will think of the word 'car' in English, and then translate it to 'la voiture' in French. Eventually, as you become more and more immersed in your French studies, you will look at a car and think of 'la voiture' before 'car'.

As French subconsciously enters your thought processes, you will find that it becomes easier to speak French confidently. It may, however, cause some confusion from time to time when you begin having thoughts in Franglais – part French and part English.

Overcome Anxiety About Speaking

Speaking a new language takes a lot of self-confidence and courage. It can be quite daunting and nerve-racking to have to speak in a different tongue in front of other people, especially if those people are native speakers. Speaking anxiety can be incredibly frustrating and can make you feel like you do not know how to say anything, in any language at all.

The first step to overcoming speaking anxiety is acknowledging that it can be a problem. It is completely natural to feel nervous when you first speak French and it is more than likely that you will make mistakes. The most important thing to keep in mind is that these beginners' jitters will not last forever.

These tips will help you prepare for speaking French and help keep speaking anxiety at bay.

o **Take a deep breath and relax**. Do not focus on what could go wrong as soon as you start speaking French. Rather, concentrate on what you do know. When you are in a relaxed mind set, you will be amazed at how much better you are able to speak the language. Remember that even native French speakers butcher their language through grammatically incorrect sentences and colloquial expressions.

o **Think before speaking.** You should not underestimate the power of thinking before you open your mouth, especially in the beginning stages of learning French. Even in your native tongue, it is a good idea to think about what you want to say and what message you want to convey. Take a few seconds to gather your thoughts and then convert them into spoken words. At the beginning, the conversation will be a bit awkward (sometimes there will be silence), so fill in the gap with some filler/conversational connector sentences.

  • Here are three good connector sentences that will give you more time to think:
  • alors = so..then…
  • laisse-moi réfléchir = let me think
  • je n'ai pas réfléchi à cela auparavant, mais = I haven't thought about it before, but ...

o **Speak slowly.** Speaking French is not a sprint race; rather, think of it as a marathon. This does not mean you should slow down and speak at a turtle's pace. It just means that you should not rush what you are trying to say. Rather, focus on the right pronunciation using liaisons and the correct sentence structure. Imagine you are speaking at an interview and want to make a good impression, rather than chatting with your friends, when you'd usually speak faster.

o **Practice to gain confidence**. Practice really does make perfect. It is unrealistic to expect to go from learning a French word one day to speaking fluently the next. You need to practice what you know and think of learning French as a continual practice. When you first learn the phrase *je m'appelle,* you will keep practicing it all throughout your French learning, because it is so commonly used. After a few days or weeks, this phrase will be perfected due to all the times you repeated it.

o **Make mistakes.** Remember that you are human, and humans do make mistakes. The first time you say something in French, it will not be perfect. But this is why you continually practice the language. When you make a mistake, such as mispronouncing a word or using the adjective in the wrong place in the sentence, learn from it. Do not let your mistakes hinder your confidence and stop you from trying. Rather, look at the mistake you made, make a mental note of it, and you likely will not repeat the same mistake twice.

Chapter 6 Review

Speaking in a new language can be quite a hair-raising scenario for a lot of people. But, like everything else, you will get better with constant practice. Below are proven ways in which you can improve your French-speaking, as discussed in this chapter:

- Listen to French podcasts or recordings, pause after a sentence or paragraph, and repeat what was said
- Record yourself speaking French
- Read out loud
- Think in French – then your thoughts will translate naturally into spoken French
- Label items around your home and say the words aloud when you see them
- Use French phrases in every day conversation, like 'good morning' or 'how are you?'
- Have conversations with native French speakers when you get the chance, and do not be self-conscious about it! Remember that the best way to learn is to hear your mistakes in conversations and have the chance for someone to correct them.

Chapter 7 –
Study Methods:
Write Like An Expert in French

*B*eing able to write in French is a great skill to have. It can be challenging to write because it requires active learning in which you have to generate your own grammatical awareness and be attuned to correct word order and sentence structure. This is a similar issue that makes speaking in a different language quite difficult. Reading and listening, on the other hand, are equally important but use a more passive brain process because the words and sentences are already created for you.

When you write in French, you are drawing upon things you have learned from all of your studies. For instance, when you write, you read over your work, speak it aloud, and listen to how it sounds. These following ideas will help you make the most of your writing skills and continually improve your written French.

The benefits of writing

Although writing may seem difficult and tedious to get right, it is a very important skill to have. Writing is used every day, more often than you may think. Think about how much you write each day in your native language - a daily reminder, an entry into your smartphone calendar, a text message, emails, and so on. These are all relevant examples of how you can use writing while learning French.

These informal ways of writing serve as an ideal alternative to speaking French. For example, if you do not have a conversation partner to practice speaking with in real time, you can send emails or text messages to a French learning partner and receive written feedback. This can often be easier to process and refer back to than oral feedback.

Write to Other People

As with improving your skills for speaking, having a network of native or fluent French speakers or other people learning French in your contacts is an invaluable learning tool. There are many ways you can connect with people and share written communication with them. Some ways include:

- If you meet French speakers or learners during your travels, exchange email details and write to each other in French.

- Check out websites such as iTalki or mylanguageexchange.com to connect with an online community of French learners and speakers.

- Have a look at forums you are interested in and write in French about topics you enjoy.

- Read blogs in French, leave comments, and ask someone to correct your French. You will be surprised how many people will be open to correcting you. Be sure to choose a popular article or a website with an active community.

Write to Yourself

Getting into the habit of writing in French on a daily basis will produce positive results in your French skills and help writing become a natural activity, rather than something you have to think strenuously about. A writing habit can be created by writing little things in French each day. It does not necessarily have to be full sentences -- just a few French words. This way, you are still familiarizing yourself with French vocabulary and committing the process of writing in French to your muscle memory.

Keep a journal

If you have a small notebook handy, each day write a few things that you did. It is best to write the date, day of the week, and month as a means to practice basic vocabulary. A journal does not have to be in-depth. Just write three bullet points about things you did during the day. Even keep a line free to write two or three emotions you felt through the day, again to practice basic vocabulary. Also, you can record details like how the weather was or what your favourite food was that day, and other small details about the day.

Write yourself daily reminders

If you are a person who needs a little help remembering what you need to do throughout your day, why not remind yourself in French and practice your writing and reading comprehension skills at the same time? Sticky notes are excellent for hand writing reminders. Smartphones are also fantastic. On most smartphones or tablets, you can add the French language to your keypad. When you open up your reminders or notes, change the language to French and type out your to-do list this way.

Change your calendar to French

Similar to giving yourself daily reminders, get in the habit of writing on your calendar, paper, or on the smartphone, in French. You can also do the same for a weekly schedule. Having these small things that you glance at regularly in French will help your brain switch languages and process things in French.

Write your shopping list in French

When you are getting ready for a big grocery shopping trip, write everything you need out in French. When you are just beginning with French, it might be best to write a bilingual shopping list so that you do not end up buying the wrong items at the store.

As you progress and have a shopping list in just French, you will be training your brain to think in French and automatically translate when you are buying the items. Being able to look at a word in English and French and simultaneously understand both languages is an excellent skill to have.

Read, Then Write

When you read something in French, you are paying attention to the word order, use of verbs or adjectives around a subject or object, different tenses, and expression and syntax. All of these things help to make a better writer, as well.

When you read something you really connect with and enjoy in French, try writing it as well. It is best to copy out writing using the old-fashioned pen and paper method, rather than typing it on a computer. This is because writing turns into muscle memory and you invariably pay more attention to the letter formation, use of accents and contractions, as well as the composition of the sentence.

When you copy something, you also fill your mind with ideas to use in your future writings. For example, if there is a line from a song you find really catchy, you can paraphrase this and reuse it one day in an essay topic or letter when writing French.

Copying out writing is a good idea also because it involves reading or listening to something first. If you have come across something during your reading and listening activities that caught your attention, keep them handy to copy out. Some ideas might include:

o Song lyrics you really like
o Passage from a book you enjoyed reading
o Inspirational and motivational quotes
o A recipe you want to try
o Information about a topic you like, such as sports or animals

Write, Then Speak

Speaking is a really important part of the proofreading process. When you re-read your writing, you are checking for grammar mistakes and spelling typos. But when you do this through speaking, you are also attuning your ears to the flow of the writing and how it sounds verbally.

When you are reading over your writing, ask yourself the following questions:

o Are the sentences too long? Should a comma be used, or a full stop to create two sentences?
o Have I used liaisons where they need to be?
o Have I missed any contractions?
o Do all the genders match? Remember to listen for feminine word endings when they need to be used.
o Do the ideas in my text flow together?
o Is the word order with nouns, verbs, and adjectives correct?

Learn 'Real' French Writing

As opposed to highly structured and formal writing in French, 'real' French writing deals with conversational and colloquial expressions that would be used in writing emails to friends or family. This is similar to speaking conversationally using authentic French phrases, rather than formal expressions from a textbook.

Idioms

These are small sayings that are used in everyday speech. Idioms provide some humour and light-hearted relief in writing. The tricky thing with idioms is that they do not translate directly into English, which is something important to keep in mind. Here are some examples of just how indirectly French idioms translate into English.

French idiom	English meaning	*Direct English translation*
Faire la tête	To sulk	*To do the head*
Être sans voix	To be speechless	*To be without a voice*
Manger sur le pouce	To grab a bite to eat	*To eat on the thumb*
Être soupe au lait	To be quick-tempered	*To be a milky soup*
Ne rien faire de ses dix doigts	To be lazy	*To do nothing with one's ten fingers*
Faire l'andouille	To do something ridiculous	*To make the sausage*
Chercher la petite bête	To look for something to complain about	*To look for the little beast*

Abbreviations

Just like English, the French language has abbreviations and ways to shorten words. These can be confusing to a non-native speaker, but learning a few can help make your writing flow better and sound less formal. These are also good to keep in mind for reading, in case you stumble across some letters that you are not sure the meaning of. Some examples of these, with English equivalents, include:

French abbreviation	Full French expression	English meaning
c-à-d	C'est-à-dire	That is, I mean
CB	Carte-bleu, carte bancaire	Debit card, bank card
Cie	Compagnie	Co. (company)
CP	Cours préparatoire	First grade (primary school)
DAB	Distributeur automatique de billets	ATM cash dispenser
É-U	États-Unis	United States of America
H	Heure	Hour – telling the time
SVP	S'il vous plait	Please
TGV	Train à grande vitesse	High speed trains
W-C	Water closet	Bathroom

How to Enhance Your Writing

Once you have a strong grasp of the grammar and syntax of sentence composition, the next step is writing in length. Whether you are writing an essay, a letter, a memoir, or just some of your thoughts, you can enhance your writing by keeping in mind some of the following tips.

Connectives

These refer to words used throughout your writing to connect ideas together. Connectives are generally best used to replace words such as 'and,' 'then,' or 'because'. Keeping a list of connectives available to refer to when writing will help you enhance the piece you are working on. Some handy connectives to keep in mind for French writing are:

French	English
Après	After
Puis / suivant	Next
Avant	Before
Souvent	Often
Aussi	Also
Ainsi	Thus
Parfois	Sometimes
Donc	Therefore
Alors	So
C'est pourquoi	That's why

Pour	In order to
En fait	In fact

Sentence openers

Having a collection of sentence openers to refer back to will make your writing much more engaging. Rather than opening every new sentence or paragraph with 'and then' or 'I think,' try some other more interesting ways to begin. Some ideas for sentence openers in French include:

French	English
D'habitude	Usually
Normalement	Normally
Le week-end	On the week-end
Il y a un an	A year ago
L'année dernière	Last year
A mon avis	In my opinion
Il faut	It is necessary
Quelquefois	Sometimes
Heureusement	Fortunately
De temps de temps	From time to time

Malheureusement	Unfortunately
Malgré	Despite

Keep sentences short

When you are writing in a foreign language, it is important not to overload a sentence. If you attempt to write a long sentence, you are at risk of making more errors and getting jumbled up in the length of it. Instead, always try to break a sentence down into smaller parts. For example, look at this sentence:

> *Demain, il fera beau et je voudrais / j'aimerais vraiment aller à la plage parce que j'adore nager.*

> *(Tomorrow, it will be sunny and I really want to go to the beach because I love swimming a lot.)*

Instead of having so many ideas in the one sentence, it can be easily broken down and made easier to both read and write. For example:

> *Demain, il fera beau. Je voudrais/ J'aimerais beaucoup aller à la plage. J'adore nager.*

> *(Tomorrow, it will be sunny. I really want to go the beach. I love swimming a lot.)*

Accept feedback and constructive criticism

When you complete any piece of writing, it is important to get feedback on it. Whether you obtain feedback from your French teacher or use a social network contact like a friend also learning French, it is an important part of improving to have objective feedback. When someone else reads your work and proofreads it, they notice minor details that you may have overlooked which can be changed to make the work better. Always remember that feedback and constructive criticism helps you grow as a French learner and these should be taken in a positive light. There is always room for improvement and mistakes and errors are the best way to develop your writing skills in another language.

You can also use websites like http://lang-8.com/, italki or any penpal website to improve your French writing.

Chapter 7 Review

Writing in French can be considered quite an intimidating feat to accomplish, especially for new learners of the language. Chapter 7 identified writing tips that might help you on your quest to learn the language, such as:

- Write to other people in French. This could be people you meet in real life or through the internet.

- Write to yourself. You can start a journal where you jot down a few French sentences each day, or you can also use French in your daily reminders, personal calendar, to-do list, or even in your shopping list.

- Arm yourself with a handy list of French idioms, acronyms, and connectives, and learn to pepper your writing with those.

Chapter 8 – Common Mistakes in the French Language and How to Fix Them

*M*istakes occur when learning any language – it is part of the process of acquiring a new skill. This chapter identifies some of the most common mistakes encountered when learning French. Fortunately, there is always a way to fix these mistakes and learn from them in the future.

Cognates/ False Friends

When French translates into English, the transition is not always a smooth process. Translations are rarely done word for word as the noun, verb, and adjective order changes. Another thing that creates difficulties during the translation process is cognates, otherwise known as "false friends."

These are words in French that are spelled similarly to or sound the same as words in English. The tricky part is that the meaning can be totally different. They lure French learners into a false sense of security as the word seems relatable to something you know in English. When they are used incorrectly in French, mistakes tend to happen.

Some common false friends to be wary of include:

French word / meaning	English word it looks like
Une librairie / bookstore	Library
La justesse / accurate, correct	Justice

L'habit / an outfit or dress	Habit
L'histoire / a story or history	History
L'humeur / mood, temperament	Humour
Le magasin / store	Magazine
La main / hand	Main
Les bras / arm	Bra
Le médecin / doctor	Medicine
Attendre / to wait	Attend
Demander / to ask	Demand

Gender Agreement

In French, words can either be masculine or feminine. Everything else in the sentence needs to be changed also in order to agree with the gender. When you are learning French, this is going to cause a minefield of mistakes. But over time, you come to know what to expect and you can begin to predict if a word is masculine or feminine.

You only have to make gender mistakes a few times before you start to notice it more. Some of the general rules regarding genders include:

Feminine

o   la, ma, ta, une = the, me, you, one/a
o   noun endings = ance, ee, esse, ière, lle, mme, nde, tion

Masculine

o   le, mon, ton, un = the, me, you, one/a
o   noun endings = ble, cle, eau, é, isme, ing, ou, x

Mistakes with gender tend to come about the most when words have dual gender meaning. For example, there are certain nouns, such as professions or animals, that can be masculine or feminine depending on the subject. Some of these include:

>   **Farmer** = le fermier / la fermière
>   **Actor/actress** = l'acteur / l'actrice (a good example of how this can happen in English too.)
>   **Cat** = le chat / la chatte
>   **Dog** = le chien / la chienne

Then, there are professions that do not change gender, no matter if the subject is male or female. There are also animals where both the male and female of the species is always referred to in the masculine, such as:

>   **Captain** = le capitaine
>   **Pilot** = le pilote
>   **Zebra** = le zèbre
>   **Bird** = l'oiseau

Remember that there are always exceptions to the rule. For example, when you refer to a friend, *amie*, the masculine possessive adjective is always "mon". So, whether the friend is a boy or a girl, you always say *mon ami(e)*. This happens any time a feminine noun starts with a vowel. Why? It is just one of those things that sound better with the liaison, and does not sound good with the usual rule of contraction. To remember this, try articulating *ma amie* or *m'amie*. It lacks the flow and intonation that the French language needs. The French language likes to sound good, so exceptions to the rule are put in place.

Cette/ce/ces

The demonstrative adjectives *ce* and *cette* are used for masculine and feminine words. They translate as 'this' or 'that'. For example, *ce garcon* means *this boy*, and *cette fille* means *this girl*. As we have previously discussed, gender agreement can cause many mistakes. This is a prime example of why this occurs for French learners.

In the plural, 'ce' becomes 'ces', which makes sense following pluralisation rules. Rather than the feminine plural of 'cette' becoming 'cettes', as the rule might suggest, it also takes the masculine form. This means that the plural of *this boy* and *this girl* becoming *those boys* and *those girls* is *ces garcons* and *ces filles*.

So, how does one know if the subject is masculine or feminine when *ces* is used in the plural form? The context of the sentence is the best indication of this. If adjectives are involved, this will tell you if the subject is masculine or feminine, based on the adjectives ending (For example, *ces filles sont très belles (those girls are very beautiful))*. Also, look at the word and its meaning, such as *fille,* which has a feminine ending and means *girls.* It is safe to make the assumption that this is a feminine word.

Pronunciation

Speaking French is challenging because mistakes are so easily made. When you have to pay attention to so many factors, such as correct word order in a sentence, the right verb conjugation, and matching the genders appropriately, the last thing you want to think about is pronunciation as well. The French language has a certain sound to it and, when pronounced correctly, it sounds wonderful. However, learners of French easily make mistakes when pronouncing certain words. These mistakes often occur because of a few tricky letters in the French alphabet.

The letter R

The "rolling" in French is notorious for creating mistakes with pronunciation for French learners. The difficulty with the French R is that it sounds nothing like the English R, or the letter R in any other language for that matter. There is only one way to get the French R perfect – and that's practice! The French R comes from the back of your throat and is pushed forward with air.

The letter H

This letter causes mistakes because it comes in two forms: the H muet and the H aspiré. The letter H is always silent in French, but it can act like a consonant or a vowel. The H aspiré acts like a consonant, so contractions and liaisons are not permitted, such as in *la halle (market)*. The H muet acts like a vowel, so contractions and liaisons must happen, such as in *j'habite (I live)*.

The letter H is more likely to cause mistakes in written French, so long as you remember in spoken French that it is always silent. This is one of the things with French that you get a feel for over time. Try memorizing some common H aspiré words for writing. When writing, say the word out loud to get a sense of whether or not it needs a contraction or liaison. If it sounds better with the contraction or liaison, then it is likely to be the H muet.

Nasal vowels

This sound can be hard for non-native French speakers to articulate. There is no equivalent to this sound in English so it is completely foreign when learning French. The nasal sound is created by pushing air through the nose and mouth. Nasal vowels are expressed when vowels are followed by the letter M or N.

As with correcting most mistakes related to learning French, practice is the key. Pronunciation takes time to develop, and it takes a long time to sound like a native French speaker. Practice, practice, and more practice is the only way to improve the mistakes you make as a beginner of French. Once you are able to identify the mistake you are making in the pronunciation of certain words and listen to how it is meant to sound, your ear and mouth will become attuned and trained to fix these mistakes.

Adjective Placement

Word order causes many mistakes to be made when learning French. These mistakes occur commonly with adjectives. This is because in English, the adjective almost always comes before the noun. In French, the general rule is that the adjective is placed after the noun. When this happens, the noun modifies the adjective and decides what gender the adjective is going to be; for instance: *les chaussures noires (the black shoes).* But there are always exceptions to this, which create mistakes.

For example, certain adjectives are placed before the noun, such as:

o   Bon (good)
o   Mauvais (bad)
o   Petit (small)
o   Grand (tall)

Even though these adjectives come before the noun, they still need to be modified to agree with the gender; for instance: *la petite chatte (the little cat).*

The meaning of an adjective can sometimes change, depending on whether it is placed before or after the noun. For example:

o   Son ancien mari = her former husband
o   Une statue ancienne = an antique statue

The only way to know these exceptions is to learn them and identify them when they happen. This can be done by reading French texts and looking out for adjectives and where they are placed. When you see the meaning change depending on the placement, make a note of it and store it in your memory.

Verbs

French verbs are not simple, especially when their translations do not match up with what we expect in English. It is always important to remember that expressions and phrases in English cannot be translated word for word into French -- otherwise, mistakes will occur.

Être, Avoir, Faire

The literal translation of *être* into English is *to be*. However, there are many expressions that use the verb *avoir (to have)* or *faire (to do/make)* to conjugate, rather than *être*. This causes mistakes for English learners because the translation makes less sense. Some examples of this include:

English	French
To be hungry	Avoir faim
To be nice weather	Faire beau
To be hot	Avoir chaud
To be thirsty	Avoid soif
To be attentive	Faire attention à

Manquer

The verb *to miss* causes many mistakes for English-speaking French learners. In French, the phrase *I miss you* is written *Tu me manques,* which literally means *you me miss*. This is a mistake created purely by word order and reflexives. A good way to remember this one is to remember it in English with the French word order by saying *you are missing to me.*

Tu and Vous

In French, there are two different ways to say 'you'. With French, *tu* and *vous* are used to refer to someone in the singular or plural tense. This seems confusing, but it actually makes things easy, unlike in English where the word *you* is used all the time. If you take the phrase *how are you?,* and ask just one person in French, you say *comment vas tu?* But if you are addressing more than one person, you say *comment allez vous?*

This is simple for singular and plural. Where it gets complicated is that *tu* and *vous* need to be used in other ways as well. When you are addressing someone you do not know or someone who is in a superior position to yourself, such as a boss or an adult, you use the *vous* form. When you are comfortable and know someone well, such as your friends, you use *tu.* The best way to avoid mixing these up is, when in doubt, use *vous.* It is formal and polite. If the person you are speaking to responds in the *tu* form, then it is a good sign you can use *tu* as well.

Capital Letters on Words

Capital letters are an important element of grammar. In English, as in French, capitalization of letters is common knowledge that you become accustomed to in your native language. It is easy to make capitalization mistakes when learning a new language because the rules can be different. This is the case between English and French.

Some instances where capital letters are used differently include:

English (always capitalised)	French (not capitalised)
I	je
Monday (and all days of the week)	lundi, mardi, mercredi etc.
January (and all months of the year)	janvier, février, mars etc.
French, English (and other languages)	le français, l'anglais

Y and En

These are adverbial pronouns that replace prepositions such as *à, chez, de plus,* and others. These can become confusing, but they are very common in French writing and spoken expression. It can be an easy mistake for French learners to use these incorrectly because they are such small letters, but they have an important meaning behind them.

The general rule with these two pronouns is:

o   Y refers to a place that has been previously mentioned, or its knowledge is implied. In English, it is normally translated as 'there'. For example: *Je vais au magasin, tu veux y aller? (*I am going to the store, do you want to go [there]?).

o   This can be problematic for English people learning French, because the word 'there' can often be left out of a sentence without it losing its meaning. But in French, the 'y' is very important and cannot be omitted. It is also confusing because the word order is jumbled up, with 'there' coming before the verb, which is not done in English.

o **En** replaces a partitive article and noun and is equivalent to 'some', 'any', or 'one' in English. For example, *j'en ai* means 'I have some', and *je n'en ai pas besoin* means 'I don't want one'. The main mistake that occurs with 'en' for English speakers learning French is the word order and placement of the word, as it comes between the preposition and verb conjugation. As with any common mistake in French, identifying the issue and practicing its formation is the best way to improve and avoid making the same mistake in the future.

Chapter 8 Review

When you know the pitfalls most learners encounter when learning French, you will be fully prepared to navigate them properly and with confidence.

- In this chapter, we looked into the most common mistakes made while learning the language, such as (1) cognates or false friends, (2) gender agreement, (3) the use of cette/ces, (4) pronunciations of the letters R, H and the nasal vowels, (5) placement of adjectives, (6) verbs, (7) tu and vous, and (8) capitalisation of letters.

- With patience and practice, and by following the tips outlined in this book, you shall soon be able to identify these errors while speaking French, and be able to actively avoid these traps.

Chapter 9 –
How To Memorize
Vocabulary and Tenses

One of the most daunting things about learning a new language is feeling so much pressure to remember everything. Sometimes it is hard enough to remember words and spellings in our native tongue, let alone a foreign language. When you place too much pressure on yourself to memorize vocabulary and tenses in French, this can become overwhelming and lead to frustrations during the learning process. When failings happen along the way and you cannot remember a simple word when you want to write or speak, you often just sigh and claim that you have a bad memory and it is impossible to remember.

When it comes to memorisation of any element of learning a language, the most important thing to remember is that **there is no such thing as a bad memory**. There are simply different learning styles and the individual brain processes memory in different ways. Perhaps your friend is able to remember twenty new words every day whereas you can barely remember two a week, even though you are attending the same amount of French classes and doing the same amount of studying. The difference is the learning style that is being used. It may work for your friend, but not for you. This does not mean you have a bad memory; it just means that you need to find a new learning style that works for your cognitive processes.

This is important to keep in mind when learning French. This chapter discusses many different strategies for remembering vocabulary and tense. You may find that one method works very well for you, whereas another does not help your progress at all. This is completely fine and it is better to use the study methods that you feel comfortable with, rather than forcing yourself to try and learn in a way that hinders your progress.

Vocabulary

Vocabulary is the basic building block of learning a language. Without an understanding of words, you cannot read, speak, or write in French. Some words are easy to learn and remember, whereas others have confusing spelling or sound very different from how they are written, making it difficult to remember them. The main thing to remember with memorizing vocabulary is to be patient and assure yourself that over time, your vocabulary will expand. Think about how you started off learning your native language – you did not know all the words you know now from birth. Vocabulary develops over time and with more exposure to the language and culture.

Set realistic goals

If you open up a French dictionary and expect to learn every word listed under the letter A section in 20 minutes, you are likely to find you will not succeed. This is not because you are bad at French or have a bad memory. It is because you are expecting too much of yourself. You need to be realistic about what you hope to achieve in a set study session. If you put too much pressure on yourself to learn too many words, your brain will not absorb the information. You can stare at the words in the letter A section of the dictionary for 20 minutes and think that you are remembering them, but an hour later you will barely remember any of the words you just read. Instead, have realistic goals and achievable expectations to inform your study sessions, and use your time wisely. A good benchmark to work with is, for every hour that you study, you can expect to learn 10-20 new words.

Keep in mind that this hour does not have to be done all at once. You can break this down throughout the week. For instance, if you give yourself 15 minutes each day to learn new vocabulary, you should expect to learn 3-7 new words. Over the week, if you study 15 minutes a day for 5 days, you will learn 25-35 new words. This is a good example of how small efforts each day, without too much pressure, can lead to positive results over time.

Learn words with context

It is good to learn individual words and it can seem appealing to simply learn a new word every day. While this is certainly a form of learning new vocabulary, the word is given little meaning without a context. If you know a new word but cannot figure out how to use it in a sentence, what is the point of learning this word?

Here are some ways that you can give your vocabulary memorization context:

Cluster words together

This process involves learning words thematically. The brain has a natural tendency to cluster together words that flow in a certain context. The way you can use this to improve remembering French vocabulary is to focus on a word theme each week. One week, focus on learning vocabulary related to the weather. The next week, learn vocabulary that relates to food.

Learn sentences

The point of remembering vocabulary words is to be able to use them in written and spoken French. Therefore, when words are given a context when you learn them, they are more likely to stick in your brain and have a practical application. Let's say you are learning words relating to food, based on the clustering strategy of working with a theme. You learn the word for apple. What colour is an apple? What does an apple taste like? What time of day do you eat an apple? These questions can inform the context for creating sentences about this new word. By doing this, you also increase or reinforce your vocabulary.

Avoid learning opposites together

It can be tempting to learn opposites when you are learning new vocabulary, such as learning *hot* and *cold* simultaneously.

This may feel like a logical pattern to follow, but it can result in vocabulary cross association. This means that when you are trying to think of the word for *cold*, your brain draws upon the knowledge from that learning stage but may find the word for *hot*, because they were learned at the same time.

A way to avoid this is to focus on the context for words instead. When you learn the word for *hot*, try to think of things that are associated with being hot. For example, think of the sun or the beach or a cup of coffee. Learn the vocabulary for these words as well as the word for hot simultaneously.

Then, in a separate study session, do the same for the word for *cold*. Word association with cold might relate to things like ice cream, snow, or freezer. Then, these words will be connected in your brain with the word for cold and this will help you remember it.

Work around the word

When you are learning French, there are likely to be some words that you just cannot remember, no matter how hard you try. Another scenario is that you know a word, but simply cannot remember it when you want to use it in a conversation. This is not the end of the world. When you cannot think of or remember a word in a conversation, here are three strategies you can use to help you:

Learn synonyms

When you learn a new word, it is also a good idea to look up one or two other words that are similar to it. This is particularly useful when it comes to adjectives. This way, if you are trying to describe a good meal that you recently ate at a restaurant and cannot think of the word for tasty, you can think of synonyms such as delicious or very good.

Describe the word you are trying to say

It can be frustrating when you are having a conversation and you think of a word you want to say, but cannot quite remember how to say it. A way to bring the word back to your memory is to describe it to your conversation partner. You might be trying to say "in the bedroom" but cannot think of the direct word. So you can work around this by saying things such as "the place where you sleep" or "where the bed is" and then your conversation partner can help you fill in the blank.

Don't be afraid to ask

When all else fails and you still cannot think of the word, simply say in French "comment dit-on déjà ___ en français" which means, "how do you say ___ in French" and the person you are talking to will be able to help you figure it out.

Analyse new words as you learn them

It is all well and good to learn new words, but if you are not paying attention to how these words are written and formed then you are missing a very good learning opportunity. The wonderful thing about words is that they often have a root. This is true for nouns, verbs and adjectives. Being aware of the root of words makes learning new vocabulary much easier. It is also reassuring to know that you mainly just have to memorize a root of a word, and from that you can add a prefix or suffix and have two additional words in your knowledge bank.

IN/IR prefix

This prefix is often added to the beginning of adjectives, adverbs, and nouns to create their opposite.

Root word	With prefix	*Meaning in English*
Acceptable	Inacceptable	*Unacceptable*
Décemment	Indécemment	*Indecently*
Rationnel	Irrationnel	*Irrational*
Régulier	Irrégulier	*Irregular*

A prefix

This prefix is added to a noun or adjective in order to create the negation.

Root word	With prefix	*Meaning in English*
Normal	Anormal	*Abnormal*
Symétrie	Asymétrie	*Asymmetry*

RE prefix

This prefix is added to verbs to create new verbs, generally meaning to do something again.

Root word	With prefix	*Meaning in English*
Marier	Remarier	*To marry again*
Sortir	Ressortir	*To go out again*
Sembler	Ressembler	*To resemble*
Entrer	Rentrer	*To return home*
Écrire	Récrire	*To rewrite*

AGE suffix

This is a suffix that is commonly added to masculine nouns or verbs to make nouns with a new meaning.

Root word	With suffix	*Meaning in English*
Jardiner	Le jardinage	*Gardening*
Raffiner	Le raffinage	*Refining*
Raser	Le rasage	*Shaving*

ENT suffix

In English, to create an adverb, the suffix *-ly* is added to an adjective. In French, the suffix *-ment* is added.

Root word	With suffix	*Meaning in English*
Heureuse	Heureusement	*Fortunately*
Rare	Rarement	*Rarely*
Général	Généralement	*Generally*
Absolu	Absolument	*Absolutely*
Vrai	Vraiment	*Truly*

ISSIME suffix

Here, the suffix makes an adjective stronger and gives it more emphasis.

Root word	With suffix	*Meaning in English*
Belle	Bellissime	*Very beautiful*

Grand	Grandissime	*Very big*
Grave	Gravissime	*Very seriously*

ÉE suffix

This suffix is added to nouns or verbs to create a new meaning and changes the gender to feminine.

Root word	**With suffix**	***Meaning in English***
Une cuillère	Une cuillerée	*A spoonful*
Une maison	Une maisonnée	*A household*
Aller	Une allée	*A walk, a path*
Un an	Une année	*A year*
Un jour	Une journée	*A day*

Read to increase your vocabulary

Reading is the key to unlocking a plethora of new words and increasing your vocabulary. When you read anything, from a novel or a newspaper to an article on the internet, you are exposing yourself to new vocabulary. This can be an ideal learning opportunity to memorize some new vocabulary. When you are reading and you come across a new word, take the time to write it down or look it up to find out its meaning.

The best way to do this is to start by reading something you are interested in. If you have an interest in sports and you choose to read an article about basketball, you will be more engaged with the topic. If you are reading this article and you find a word that you do not know, you will be inclined to look it up and find out its meaning. Once you know what it means and reread the sentence, you have a context for this new word. Finally, because you like basketball, the next time you play or watch a basketball game, you remember this new word you learned because it is relevant to something you are interested in and, therefore, fits into your real life.

Use visual representations

When you associate words with images as you learn a new language, you are more likely to remember it. Pictorial representation is a very strong study method and has many benefits in the early stages of learning new vocabulary.

Flashcards are an effective way to enhance your vocabulary memorisation with visual aids. Flashcards can be bought at shops or printed online. They can even be accessed through the internet, at websites such as this: Flashcards online http://www.frenchverbtest.com/

Technology has made learning languages and memorizing vocabulary even easier with the introduction of apps on smartphones. Some top apps to learn French visually include:

Memrise http://Memrise.com/

Busuu https://play.google.com/store/apps/details?id=com.busuu.android.fr

Babbel https://play.google.com/store/apps/details?id=com.babbel.mobile.android.fr

Visual learning with vocabulary tends to focus on singular words. Remember that this chapter has previously discussed the importance of learning words within a context. Flashcards and pictorial representations are a good introductory lesson to exposing yourself to French vocabulary. To get more out of learning this way, you should try speaking or writing a sentence using the word that shows up on the flashcard. This will enhance your studies and reinforce the word you are learning.

Pay attention to English and French cognates

Cognates are words that look and sound alike in two different languages. Between French and English, there are a whole bunch of cognates. Some of these cognates have the same meaning and are often referred to as *true friends/true cognates* because they make memorizing vocabulary much easier. Some true cognates include:

French word	English word	*Both meaning*
Action	Action	*Something you do*
Adorable	Adorable	*Cute, sweet*
Direction	Direction	*Where something is headed*
Herbivore	Herbivore	*A plant eater*
Machine	Machine	*A technological item*
Possible	Possible	*Something achievable*

However, there are also many cognates that have different meanings between French and English. These are called *false friends* because they are like hidden traps for English speakers learning French. When you see a word in French that looks or sounds just like an English one, you easily assume it has the same meaning. But false friends mean something different in French. Some examples of false cognates are:

French word	*French meaning*	English word	*English meaning*
Actuellement	*At the present time*	Actually	*Really, in fact*
Attendre	*To wait for*	Attend	*To attend*

Cent	*Hundred*	Cent	*Referring to currency*
Demander	*To ask for*	Demand	*To demand*
Éventuelle-ment	*Possibly, if need be*	Eventually	*It will happen later*
Formidable	*Great, terrific*	Formidable	*Dreadful, fear-some*
Quitter	*To leave*	Quit	*To stop, to give up*

The only thing to remember with false cognates is that the pronunciation often changes, although they are spelled the same. Also keep in mind that in French, the spelling of certain words changes depending on whether it is a masculine or feminine word. This alters the relationship with French and English cognates.

Tense

Start in the present

Learning the tenses of verbs in French can be overwhelming. From present to future perfect and past perfect to the subjunctive, it can be easy to get lost in all these different conjugations. The best starting point is to focus only on the present. This will give you confidence and a sense of comfort with a very useful tense. The present is used most commonly and will be very practical in conversational and written French.

The present is also an ideal starting point as it forms the basis of some compound verbs, such as *le futur*. Once you know the present and you know it well, conjugating verbs into the past and future will not seem as intimidating.

Read aloud

When you are reading a book or an article in French, you will invariably come across conjugations of verbs. It is good to see them written, but take it one step further and say it aloud. This gives you practice in linking the written conjugation with how it is spoken, while you are listening to yourself say it at the same time. This taps into all elements of learning a language and will help the conjugation stick in your brain.

Write them down

During your study sessions, take some time to write out the conjugation of different verbs. When beginning, it is good to write out just the present conjugation. Once you have this comfortably memorized, move on to writing out the past and present conjugations as well. While writing, if you are feeling confident, also say them out loud. Try to write it out at least five times and say it aloud at the same time. This form of repetition will train your muscle memory through writing and your oral memory through speaking, as well as your auditory memory by listening to yourself speak. This will help you memorize the conjugations effectively.

Get to know the rule, then learn the exceptions

In French, and in any language for that matter, there are always exceptions to the grammar rules. This can be daunting, but just remember to learn the rule first and then worry about the exceptions later. We already know with verb conjugations in French that there are three verb endings: *er, ir, and re. Er* verbs are generally always regular, *ir* verbs are mostly regular, and *re* verbs are generally always irregular. This helps inform conjugations as well.

Tenses

- For conjugations, there are four tenses to focus on:
- *Present:* an action happening now, i.e.: I am

- *Passé composé:* the past perfect, something that is complete, i.e.: I did, I have done
- *Imparfait:* the past, not specific to a time, i.e.: I was doing, I used to
- *Futur simple:* I will do

The passé composé tense uses an auxiliary verb when conjugating. You can remember this because they are made up of two words: *passé composé,* and this means that they need two words to make up the tense.

Er verbs – manger (to eat)

	Present	Past (passé composé)	Past (imparfait)	Future (futur simple)
Je	mange	ai mangé	mangeais	Mangerai
Tu	manges	as mangé	mangeais	Mangeras
Il/elle/on	mange	a mangé	mangeait	Mangera
Nous	mangeons	avons mangé	mangions	Mangerons
Vous	mangez	avez mangé	mangiez	Mangerez
Ils/elles	mangent	ont mangé	mangeaint	Mangeront

Ir verbs – venir (to come)

	Present	Past (passé composé)	Past (imparfait)	Future (futur simple)
Je	viens	suis venu	venais	Viendrai

Tu	viens	es venu	venais	Viendras
Il/elle/on	vient	est venu	venait	Viendra
Nous	venons	sommes venus	venions	Viendrons
Vous	venez	êtes venus	veniez	Viendrez
Ils/elles	viennent	sont venus	venaient	viendront

Re verbs – entendre (to hear)

	Present	Past (passé composé)	Past (imparfait)	Future (futur simple)
Je	entends	ai entendu	entendais	entendrai
Tu	entends	as entendu	entendais	entendras
Il/elle/on	entend	a entendu	entendait	entendra
Nous	entendons	avons entendu	entendions	entendrons
Vous	entendez	avez entendu	entendiez	entendrez
Ils/elles	entendent	ont entendu	entendaient	entendront

Chapter 9 Review

Vocabulary is the foundation you must properly build on in order to learn a whole new language. However, each language has hundreds of thousands (even millions) of words that you need to recognize and understand. It can be such a daunting task memorizing all the words, but before you start buckling under the pressure of learning too many French words and tenses, STOP and give yourself a break. If the usual ways of memorizing is seriously causing trouble in your brain, consider other methods or hacks that you can use to learn – and retain – vocabulary faster.

Try some of the simple tricks below. These might be just what you need to assist you:

1. **List and carry.** List all the words you want to memorize and take the list with you everywhere. Every time you have a spare moment, review the list. Repeat the process until it sticks.

2. **Associate a feeling or thought to the word.** When you read a word, what thoughts does it trigger in your mind? What pictures does it paint in your brain? What do you think it looks like or sounds like? If you can attach a feeling or relate a thought to it, the word you are trying to remember will most likely stick in your mind. But be as natural as possible and avoid coming up with complicated word associations. Use the first thing that comes to your mind, otherwise the plan will backfire and you will be trying to remember both the word and the thought you are trying to associate it with. Not fun at all.

3. **Be creative!** Your imagination can do wonders for you when learning new vocabulary words. Create a short, humorous story about the words you are learning and why they are translated the way they are.

4. **Use music**. If you are the musical type, memorizing will come naturally to you if it is set to some background music. Put a tune to the vocabulary you are trying to memorize, or maybe even turn it into a rap song. Record the clip and then listen to it. The words will be stuck in your brain in no time.

5. **Take note of stressed syllables.** For some reason, the human brain can pick up stressed sounds faster. So when trying to memorize a word, focus more attention on the stressed syllable.

Remember, different brains work differently. Try to find the right fit for your learning style, and do not be afraid to experiment to find what works best for your memory.

Chapter 10 –
Study Guide: A Typical Day for a
Language Learner

How much French should you be looking at each day?

*I*t can be tempting to think that the more time you spend studying French, the better your results will be and the faster you will improve. However, this is not necessarily the case. It is more a matter of quality versus quantity when it comes to studying a language. If you spend a short amount of time really focusing on what you are learning, you are more likely to retain the information and absorb new facts. It also depends entirely on your work schedule and life balance as to how much French you can study per day.

A good way to fit French into your daily life is to use immersion techniques. This study method allows you to include French in your day as you go about your everyday life. Below is a rough guide as to how much French you should try to immerse yourself in, covering all the different areas of learning a new language.

Listening skills
10 minutes per day

Listening is a crucial skill to have when learning French. Being able to listen to another language helps you develop your own speaking skills as you hear the formation of sentences, as well as developing your comprehension so that you understand what is being said in a conversation.

Listening can be enhanced by playing audio books, listening to music or radio, or even recording yourself speaking in French and listening to it throughout the day. A good amount of time to spend listening to French is ten minutes over the course of the day. This can be done all in one sitting, or broken up throughout different stages of the day.

Grammar skills
15 minutes per day

The foundation of learning French is understanding the grammatical structures of the language. Grammar encompasses all areas of how the language is made up and it is the entire system that tells learners the rules they need to know to understand it. Grammar includes things such as verb conjugations, parts of speech, tenses, prepositions, nouns, verbs, adjectives, adverbs, and pronouns.

Grammar can be a challenging area to learn in a new language because the rules can become very confusing. It can also be frustrating when there are constantly exceptions to the rule. The main thing to remember when learning grammar is to just focus on one small area at a time. If you spend fifteen minutes a day learning all about verb conjugations, you will stay focused on this important area. The next day, if you learn all about prepositions and the general rules for these in French, you will build upon your previous knowledge of verb conjugations. Grammar is accumulative and the pieces always work together, but it is important not to inundate yourself with too many elements of grammar in one sitting.

Writing practice and vocabulary
20 minutes per day

Writing is a skill that you use more than you think in a foreign language. Often, it is easy to believe that you hardly ever need to write anything in French. However, if you think about how much written communication you do in your first language, such as sending emails or typing text messages, you begin to realize how much of a practical skill it is in French as well.

You can practice writing in many different ways and spread the twenty minutes of writing across the day in a variety of tasks. Things such as making a to-do list, a shopping list, or writing reminders in French is a good place to start. Also, looking at articles or books that you are interested in and reading over these with a pen and paper handy to write down new words is a great activity. If you do this, aim to write down 5 or 10 new words, including verbs, to practice the written form of French. It can also be helpful to keep a journal or diary and write down a few things that you did that day or some thoughts you had, or even writing a short essay or story once you feel more confident with French.

Reading
15 minutes per day

The first thought when it comes to reading may be that it only applies to reading novels, but this is not the case. You are constantly reading everywhere you go throughout the day, everything from street signs to the menu at restaurants. Reading is a vital skill that can be practiced easily throughout your day and you will likely spend more than fifteen minutes reading French without even noticing it.

When you are looking for things to read, consider reading blogs and news articles on your computer or smartphone during your lunch break. Having a French or bilingual novel on your bedside table can be ideal for some bedtime reading. Also, program your phone or computer language to French so that you are constantly seeing French words whenever you are looking at the screen.

If you have contacts who are French or other friends who are learning French, get in the habit of emailing them regularly. This is ideal for practicing your reading comprehension as well as your written skills. It is also fun to have a French network so that you will feel more motivated to continually improve your French knowledge and have a practical application for it.

How to Include French in Your Daily Routine

This is a general outline you can use as a guideline for including French in your daily routine. Of course, the activities and time frames will vary based on your own personal circumstances and schedule.

Morning

7am: *Wake up.* Set your alarm to a French song or radio station so the first thing your brain hears is French.

7.15am: *Breakfast.* While eating breakfast, open up a language-learning app on your smartphone such as memrise or duolingo and practice some vocabulary.

8am: *Commute to work.* Have a French song or podcast playing during your drive, or read a French article on your phone if you are taking public transportation.

Afternoon

1pm: *Lunch break.* Read a French article, newspaper, or blog while eating lunch. Alternatively, write down in a journal in French some thoughts for the day, or make a to-do list.

2.45pm: *Coffee break.* While having a cup of coffee, open up your smartphone and use memrise or duolingo, or play a French vocab game.

5pm: *Commute home.* Reward yourself for a hard day's work and listen to some fun songs in French that you know and enjoy, or read a book on the train that you find easy and fun.

Evening

8pm: *Study time.* After dinner, set aside a solid study block session with specific points you want to study for each day, such as grammar or verb tenses. Give yourself 20-30 minutes of solid study, and continue if you are feeling comfortable and happy with your progress.

9pm: *Relax and let your brain rest.* Maybe watch a French YouTube clip or a funny video to unwind a bit.

10pm: *Bed time.* Continue reading a French book that you have been enjoying or watch a French film as you fall asleep.

Chapter 10 Review

The quality of time you spend learning amounts to so much more than the quantity of time you put into it. Rather than flood your daily schedule with studying French, try inserting fun French activities in your daily routine. Weaving tasks like listening to a French song on your way to work or reading a French article while eating lunch are a less obtrusive way of immersing yourself into the language.

This chapter broke down the details of how much time you should allocate to learning French each day, as shown below:

·   10 minutes for listening skills

·   15 minutes for grammar skills

·   20 minutes for writing practice and vocabulary

·   15 minutes for reading

Print a copy of the schedule included in this chapter and use it to guide you in your daily routine. It is not a one-size-fits-all thing, but it will definitely help you immerse yourself in French daily.

Chapter 11 –
For Intermediate and Advanced
Learners – Do You "Plateau?"

What is plateauing?

When you start learning a language, you are filled with motivation to achieve all the goals you set for yourself. This is a wonderful feeling that drives you to keep moving forward and continually learn the language. However, as you progress and become more competent in the language, you are likely to reach a plateau.

A plateau is a natural stage in the process of learning a language. This is the point where you are good at the language, but you could be better. Your motivation begins to dwindle and you are less inclined to keep achieving because you are already at a comfortable point.

Why do you plateau?

There are many things that cause a plateau, but the main factor is the time you have invested in learning the language. Other things that can cause a plateau include:

- **When you no longer stick to the same habits you enforced in the beginning.** These can include things such as including French in your daily routine and doing something French each day. As you become complacent with your progress, you often become less strict with daily immersion.

- **When you reach an autonomous stage in your language learning.** This is likely to happen when you start to attend fewer classes or have your work checked less often by someone else.

This therefore means that you receive less feedback, or you do not respond as much to feedback because you feel confident with the stage you are at.

- **When you begin to focus less on your technique and pay less attention to verb conjugations and sentence structure.** This often means that you are becoming increasingly fluent with French, particularly when speaking. But it is important to keep paying attention to the correct verbal formation of sentences and words so that you do not lose your technique.

- **When you no longer set long-term goals, similar to how you lose focus with your habits.** In the beginning, the long-term goal of learning French is to be able to read, write, and speak fluently, and comfortably maintain conversations. When this is achieved, it can be tempting to neglect the grammatical foundations of the language and speak or write more casually.

How do you get over plateauing?

A well-known quote from Albert Einstein defines madness as "doing the same thing over and over and expecting different results." This is essentially the problem that one experiences when the plateau stage is reached. This is to be expected and is just a natural part of the process of learning a language. When you plateau, you have become good at speaking French and have achieved many of the goals you set for yourself along the way. The difficult part is maintaining the motivation you had in the beginning to continue moving forward.

There are many things you can do in your approach to learning French that will help motivate you to continue progressing. It is important to remember, as always, to find something that works for you and try a few different options to regain motivation to push past the plateau.

Understand that there is no one-size-fits-all approach

The key to overcoming a plateau in your French language development is to change your approach. Language learning is highly subjective, so there is no one-size-fits-all approach to progressing successfully. The good thing about this is that it means there are many different ways to learn, and you can continuously change your own learning.

What you need to do is recognize how you learn and focus on strategies that make learning French appealing and motivating for you. Do not force yourself to study in ways that you dislike, as this will just hinder your progress.

Identify any problems you face

Do you struggle with stringing full sentences together? Do you have difficulties with grammatical word order? Or do you tend to lose focus with writing and make a lot of spelling errors? Each individual faces his or her own personal difficulties when learning a new language. This is just part of the process of taking on a second language.

However, these problems can often contribute to the plateau stage and they can be a big reason for losing motivation to move forward. It is easy to begin thinking, *If I don't know it by now, I'm never going to get better at it.* This is not true. By identifying and owning the things that cause major problems in your learning, you can really focus on them better. This will help you move beyond the plateau and progress forward by overcoming one difficulty at a time.

What you need to do is get to know your weaknesses and embrace them as positive learning goals. Once you know where you need to improve, you will be able to focus on these areas for improvement.

Deal with big issues first

There are always going to be little things that crop up along the way and cause stumbling blocks when learning French. One that many learners of a second language face is getting annoyed at the little things as they are learning rather than focusing on the bigger issues. For example, a common thing French learners do is use awkward fillers like 'umm' or 'err' when unsure of what word to use. This can cause a lot of frustration when trying to speak French. However, there is no point in trying to deal with this issue first because this awkward stumbling filler is part of a bigger issue, which is that you need to increase your vocabulary.

To move past this point of the plateau stage, it is important to identify the little things that frustrate you and hinder your progress, and see what bigger issue they are connected to. Once the bigger issue is resolved, you can then move forward and the little issues will sort themselves out along the way.

What you need to do is understand that there is a learning problem behind the little mistakes you make – take a look at the bigger picture.

Seek out other French speakers

One way you are never going to continually improve and stay at the plateau stage is by not using your French skills. The simple fact is that if you do not use it, you will lose it. It is, therefore, important to stay connected with other French speakers and learners. Over the course of learning French, you will have met a number of people like yourself who are keen to engage themselves with the French language. These people are highly important in your motivation to keep up your French skills. By having short conversations, texting, emailing, or communicating in other ways with this type of network, you will regularly use your French skills and continually learn.

Also, look for ways to engage with French in the world around you. Most cities have a decent French cafe or bakery where you might be able to practice some French with the waiter or cashier. Another good idea is to check out the cinema to see if there are any French films playing and watch those in order to practice your listening skills as well as meet other people interested in French culture and language.

What you need to do is give your French skills real life value and find new ways to put them into practice.

Continue to immerse yourself with French

The whole point of learning French is to have another language to use in your life. Being able to speak another language is an invaluable skill for a plethora of reasons. When you continue doing small immersion tasks with French, even when you are feeling confident and comfortable with the language, you will be constantly consolidating a range of skills you have learned. This will mean that your French will always keep improving and it will become second nature for you.

Take some of the habits you created in the beginning of your French learning and keep them up. At this stage when you plateau, you have learned so much and have such a wider range of skills. You can use these to improve upon your habits and have a more in-depth connection with French in your everyday life, which will feel more effortless now that you are familiar with how the language is made up.

What you need to do is use the things you love about French and combine them with your hobbies and interests to effortlessly make each day a little bit French.

Chapter 11 Review

Sooner or later, at some point in your study of the French language, you will encounter a plateau. This happens for a lot of reasons and it is quite common when learning a language. The good news is, knowing and understanding this stage is part of solving the problem.

This chapter focused on the different ways in which you can rise above the hurdle and continue pushing yourself forward despite reaching the plateau in your learning process.

Some key points:

o You plateau for a number of reasons, but mainly it is because you have already invested a considerable amount of time in learning and you have already accomplished the goals you have set for yourself previously.

o You can get over a plateau by re-energising yourself and maintaining the motivation for learning that might have waned at this point.

o When you reach the plateau, it is time to change your approach.

o Identify problems you encountered while learning the language. Those might be the key reasons why you have reached the plateau and are therefore stuck in the proverbial rut.

o Continue immersing yourself in French. This will help in overcoming the plateau you are finding yourself in.

o Use what you have learned. Remember, if you do not use it, you will lose it.

Chapter 12 –
Resources For Hacking/
Accelerating the Language

Cheat Sheet for the Basics of French Grammar/Pronunciation/Words/Tense...

When you make positive progress quickly when learning French, you feel a great satisfaction and motivation to keep moving forward with your learning goals. It can feel like a long and burdensome journey when you think about how far you have to go in terms of becoming fluent in French. Fortunately, there are many things you can do throughout the process to accelerate your learning, and there are some great language learning hacks you can put into practice to help you progress faster.

What is the secret to hacking your French learning?

The simplest way to 'hack' learning French is to implement learning habits every day. Throughout the process of learning French you will have developed numerous little French habits, from listening to French music or radio to writing your to-do lists and notes in French. These habits are instrumental in accelerating your language learning development and will make big differences when you do them each day. The best way to maximize these learning habits is to ensure they are something you enjoy and you do them so much that your day feels strange without this form of French immersion.

What is the most important thing for your progress?

Consistency is equally important as immersion when it comes to hacking learning French. Whatever stage of learning French you are at, ensure that your learning and immersion with French is consistent and you will notice that development happens much faster. This chapter will outline some handy language learning hacks to complement your studies. Remember that your formal study should remain consistent and these hacks are just here to quicken the process.

Memorise the basics

There are some phrases that you will need to know and that you will use again and again. These are considered the basics, and include the following:

- o Greetings ('my name is ____', 'how are you?')
- o Answers to basic questions ('I am good,' 'I live in/I am from,' 'I am __ years old')
- o Basic questions ('where is the ____?', 'what time is it?', 'how much is ____?')
- o Days of the week
- o Months
- o Numbers

Example cheat sheet: http://www.cheatography.com/tag/languages/

An easy way to remember these is to create vocabulary cheat sheets and keep them easily accessible each day. For example, sticking these cheat sheets on the outside of the shower or beside the bathroom mirror is a good way to ensure that you will view them each day and be able to practice easily. Once these basic phrases are cemented in your memory, they will be easy to recall in conversation and will help boost your confidence.

Speak from day one

From the beginning of your French studies, you should endeavour to speak as much French as you can. Remember, it is important to have an understanding of the way words need to be pronounced and the formation of words. When it comes to speaking, perfection is more important than pace. This means that you should master your pronunciation of the words before attempting to speak quickly. You can do this by focusing on keywords and practicing these again and again until they sound correct. Speaking from day one will help accelerate your skills as well as improve your comprehension in all areas of French.

Make the most of cognates

Between French and English, there are many words that share the same spelling and often the same meaning. These words are generally pronounced differently, but are easy to recognise by sight and can be understood between the two languages in conversation. As discussed in previous chapters, there are cognates that have different meanings, otherwise known as 'false friends,' and these are words that you, of course, need to be aware of.

True cognates, however, are an excellent cheat to hack French. These are basically free vocabulary building blocks that will accelerate your French vocabulary and enhance your conversations. To help yourself remember cognates, it is a good idea to write down a list of words that have the same meaning between English and French and memorize these. You will find that if you start using these early on in the process of learning French, they will become commonly used words and will be handy to rely on when you are struggling to think of what word to use.

Start with the present tense

As with any language, French has different tenses of speech. When it comes to learning verb conjugations, it can be overwhelming to memorize the present, past, and future tenses as well as the moods that come along with these, such as the imperfect, conditional, and subjunctive tenses.

To make accelerated progress with French, always start by learning the present tense first. The present tense gives you a lot of conversational skills and comprehension for reading and writing, so it is the best starting point. Memorizing the present tense is a handy language-learning hack because it is always a good thing to fall back on when you are unable to think and conjugate another tense on the spot.

http://www.memorymentor.com/french_er.htm

Focus on modal verbs

Verbs are fundamental to speaking and writing French, as well as to understanding what is being said in conversations. There are obvious verbs that you need to learn and memorise at the beginning stages of your French:

o Être – to be
o Faire – to do/to make
o Avoir – to have
o Aller – to go

Once these verbs are memorized, they will be used commonly and frequently in your French practice. After you have these under your belt, the next most important verbs to focus on include modal verbs.

Modal verbs are verbs that express something that is necessary, or something that is a possibility. They are commonly used and add dynamics to your speech. They are an excellent learning hack to accelerate your conversational skills and enhance what you are trying to say. Some handy modal verbs to memorize include:

o Pouvoir – can, in the present tense: *je peux aider*
o Devoir – must, in the present tense: *je dois partir*
o Vouloir – want, in the present tense: *je veux un bonbon*
o Vouloir – would, in the present conditional tense: *je voudrais aller*

Perfect your pronunciation

Speaking French in general is good, but speaking with correct pronunciation is much better and this should be the ultimate aim of learning French. When you begin learning French, speaking from day one is a wise idea. However, before you start speaking, you should be aware of what sounds need to be pronounced properly for the best results.

The main sounds to focus on when it comes to pronunciation include:

o   The rolling R
o   Vowel combinations
o   Letters with accents
o   Nasal vowels
o   H aspiré and H muet
o   Silent S

Do not underestimate the importance of adverbs

To accelerate the amount of words you have stored away in your French vocabulary, a great learning hack is to focus on adverbs. The great thing about adverbs is how versatile they are. An adverb essentially describes the action of a verb; therefore, the root of an adverb comes from an adjective. In French, the general rule with adverbs is that they end in 'ment', just like in English where they end in 'ly'.

The reason learning adverbs can enhance your vocabulary so much is that you actually learn an adjective as well as an adverb. For example, when you learn the adjective *normal* to describe something, you can implement the rule for adverbs and turn it into *normalement* and you automatically have a new word incorporated into your vocabulary.

Adverbs are also important in written and spoken French because they add certain dynamics to a sentence. Including an adverb in a sentence can add emphasis, emotion, and affect to describe what is taking place.

For a list of adverbs, refer to the bonus section.

Attune your ears to liaison

One of the most common complaints in understanding spoken French is that it sounds too fast. What learners of French soon realize is that it is not the pace of the language that causes difficulties, but rather the way the words blend together. This is called liaison and it occurs in words that end with an S and begin with a vowel. The S sound carries over and joins up with the vowel, such as in *parlez-vous anglais.* The Z sound that this liaison creates makes it harder to distinguish the sounds and separate the words, especially in longer sentences in French.

To accelerate your French listening skills and comprehension, start by attuning your ears to the liaison and always be prepared for it. You can do this by first reading French words and then listening to audio or repeating them aloud to visually see the liaison. Once you recognize words by sight that end in S and are used to hearing them being said, you will notice it in speech and be able to identify it much easier. Being able to separate the liaison into two words makes it much easier to follow the flow of the sentence and have better comprehension of what is being said.

HACKING THE FINAL CONSONANT SOUND: Be Careful!

In French pronunciation, the FINAL consonants are usually silent, but a widely known rule is the CRFL or the "careful" consonants. The rule states that in most cases, when a word ends in C, R, F, or L, the last consonant is voiced, and not silent as is the norm in French words.

But since the world is far from perfect and even exceptions to the rules have another set of their own exceptions, things can be quite tricky. So, be careful, but do not forget the CRFL rule.

HACKING THE ADJECTIVE PLACEMENTS: Use BAGS!

In English, an adjective is placed before the word it is describing. This is not the case in French. Most French adjectives appear after the noun it describes. Still, not everything works this way since there are adjectives that do not follow this placement. One hack you can use to quickly identify the exceptions to this rule is the "BAGS adjectives". BAGS adjectives refer to B – Beauty, A – Age, G – Good and bad, and S – Size. Adjectives belonging to these categories are placed before the noun it describes. This is why you say "une jolie fille" and "un bon enfant" instead of the other way around.

HACKING DIFFICULT PRONUNCIATIONS: Try Back-chaining

Back-chaining is an ingenious technique used when teaching pronunciation of difficult polysyllabic words. This trick proves to be quite helpful when learning foreign languages and is even used in classical singing where clarity of the words and sounding impressive is highly necessary. The method is quite simple: you just begin pronouncing the last syllable first and work your way back to the beginning of the word. For example, let's try the word Rendezvous.

- -vous
- -dez vous
- -rendez vous

You can use this method for phrases and sentences too, but you still need to be mindful of liaisons and silent letters.

PRONUNCIATION HACKS USING IPA

The International Phonetic Alphabet was created by a group of French and British linguists with the purpose of documenting and describing every possible sound in every language. Being familiar with the IPA is actually a powerful hack in learning different sounds in different languages. Armed with an understanding of IPA, foreign languages can be a lot easier to learn as it allows you to identify sounds faster and pronounce new words easier. To use this hack in learning French, compare similar words (such as true cognates) in both French and English and notice how the specific sounds vary. For native English speakers learning French, pay special attention to the A and U sounds, as French has rounded vowel sounds that do not exist in English, in the same manner that Spanish speakers should take note of J and U sounds.

Learn IPA: Compare with your own language and see how French and your language are different on some specific sounds (for English speakers, pay attention to the A/U; for Spanish speakers, pay attention to J and U).

CONCLUSION

"The secret of getting ahead is getting started. The secret of getting started is breaking your complex overwhelming tasks into small manageable tasks, and starting on the first one."
-- Mark Twain

French is a beautiful language, and learning it could open doors you never knew existed. But as new learners collectively gripe about how hard learning French can be, I hope this book has chased that idea away and, instead, helped you adopt a positive mind set to approach learning as the fun, enriching activity that it is.

With all the practical tips and advice, simplified grammar rules, and study methods discussed in this study book, I hope that it will serve its purpose in helping you navigate each bump in your road to learning French.

Each chapter is fully designed with language learners' needs in mind. The chapter on motivation and habit addresses the common concern in learners' lagging motivations and how to find a way around these inevitable issues. The chapter on myths is included to address the most pressing concerns of the usual French language learner, and to drive the point that most language myths are just that – simply myths that can be debunked. Then there are the study methods to improve your listening, reading, speaking, and writing skills. All those are a product of hands-on teaching experience as well as years of endless study about what works and what does not work.

We also talked about the common mistakes in learning French and the ways to fix them. In the last few chapters you will find some of the most brilliant language hacks for learning French. You are also provided with a quick peek at what a typical language learner's day should look like – complete with a fun routine

CONCLUSION

for daily immersion.

As with all things in life, however, everything boils down to you and how you make use of all the resources you have at your fingertips.

The key point I'm driving here? **START TODAY.**

No matter what your situation or level of learning is, act now while the proverbial iron is still hot. Go download apps like duolingo, start listening to a podcast, or visit my website for more resources. As you go along, remember to keep this study guide close to you and refer to it each time you encounter a new set of difficulties.

To help you further in your French language journey, I would be grateful to assist you in any way I can. You can drop by my website, www.talkinfrench.com. There, you can find all the resources you need to learn and embrace French – podcasts, eBooks, fun articles, lifestyle topics, and many other resources, all targeting different levels of learning.

If you have any requests, do not hesitate to contact me at contact@talkinfrench.com. It will be awesome to hear from you. I will keep this study guide up-to-date with your suggestions, questions, and requests.

Bonne chance!
Frédéric Bibard

Toolbox to learning French

To back you every step of your language journey, here are some carefully curated online tools, apps, and learning aids that you can make use of to supplement your core study.

Vocabulary

Memrise is an awesome online learning tool with a wealth of courses shared by its community. Developed by a pair of experts (a memory genius and a neuroscientist), Memrise uses a Spaced Repetition System to help you memorise vocabulary. This means that the software will repeatedly show you words in a loop to ask if you remember their meaning. Each word will be presented to you just before you would be assumed to forget it. This is one of the most effective ways to learn vocabulary. You can easily download this app for some on-the-go vocabulary memorisation.

Anki uses spaced repetition flashcard system like _Memrise_, though this program gives you more flexibility and you have to enter the words and sentences yourself. The app is also easily downloadable on your computer or smartphone.

Tatoeba is a collaborative online platform that allows you to easily find example sentences from all languages. You can join the community by contributing sentences from your own native language too.

Reverso an online translation site that also has also a similar section called context.

Wordreference is my favourite online French dictionary. It contains a huge amount of words and you can ask for help on the forum if you don't understand something or couldn't find a definition.

With the limitless power of the internet right at your finger-tips, you can find the definition, synonyms, usage and pronuncia-tion of almost any word online within seconds. Even better, most of these tools, including WordReference, are FREE. It really is a win-win situation for language learners. However, this said a physical copy of a dictionary is always useful to have in a class-room or on a desk.

Grammar

Grammar can be quite tricky, but with the help of various on-line resources, things should be a lot easier for language learners like yourself. Below are some of the most useful.

French About contains lots of useful content to better under-stand French grammar and supplement your learning. From study guides, grammar lessons, vocabulary, and all types of con-tent related to French – this site has for a great deal to offer you.

Talk in French My very own website has a verity of grammar topics that you can use as a valuable resource. Visit the grammar section of the website to access these lessons.

Bon Patron is an online grammar and spelling checker that will alert you to any mistakes. Simply paste a French text into the box on the site and click the button.

Nonetheless, as with every other topic under the sun, _Google_ is often your best friend. I find that googling a problem usually gets you answers to even the most obscure questions. Should you prefer a physical grammar book, however, _French Grammar: A Complete Reference Guide_ has many positive reviews.

Practice speaking

Language is one of those things that "if you don't use it, you'll lose it!" Practice is an essential part of the language learning pro-cess. To help you in this, here are some tools that make it easy for you to find native French speakers to practice with.

Interpals is an ideal website if you are looking for someone to practice French with. It's easy to sign up and you could make some great friends from all over the world in no time.

Italki is a social network and educational website for language learners. You can use the website to practice writing and get it corrected by native speakers, as well as to find private teachers and native speakers to communicate in French with.

Couchsurfing This is another social network that you could use to supplement your French study. Couchsurfing is a community of travellers who regularly organise meetings, and chances are, there is probably one near you. The meetings are great opportunities to meet French speakers to practice with. I often use them to meet German speakers and it's always fun and interesting.

Meetup.com is a website with 21 million members, whose goal is to help people organise themselves into groups and communities. Here you can find lots of language exchange meetings to participate in.

Lang8 is another online language learning platform you can use to connect with native speakers. This is another great place to visit if you want any writing corrected. Simply post a text in French and wait for corrections by native French speakers. All you have to do in return is to correct other people's texts.

French courses

The internet is chock-full of language courses, ones that are readily available for you anytime you like. Some of the best I found online are listed below. Feel free to browse these courses.

Assimil This is a French company that produces language lessons with high-quality dialogue, great recordings and some basic grammar explanations. This is one of the best and cheapest courses you could find. Despite this, due to its simple format that uses books and recording, you will need to find a way to keep yourself motivated. This will do wonders if you're the type who likes to learn on your own, but if you prefer to feel like a part of a community, you'd be better off with a course like *Babbel*.

Babbel: More than just a language course, *Babbel* is an online community of learners that utilises language tools and innovative technology. Here you will find high-quality dialogue, recordings, a SRS tool, and you can also find a French conversation partner to practice with. This offers less flexibility than *Assimil* but would be better if you like to feel part of a community.

Duolingo: This fun and free website adopts a different approach to language learning, bringing gaming and technology together to create an innovative learning technique. With each bite-sized lesson, you can improve your listening and speaking and do some translation exercises. You can also download the app to take it with you on your travels.

French today is another good resource for you to check out. You can find good quality lessons as well as audio lessons and books for all study levels.

Talk In French: You should, of course, also check out my website Talk In French. Lessons are around 15 to 20 minutes and will fit neatly in your daily schedule. The course is still a work in progress and should available in July 2015. We are working hard to ensure fun and helpful content for all kinds of learners; so make sure to visit every now and then for updates.

Pronunciation

A common problem area for new learners, pronunciation can be a pain to learn. Though with lots of practice and a handy guide to help you, it should be easier.

Forvo is an online database boasting of containing all words in all languages pronounced by native speakers.

Rhinospike If the word or sentence you are looking for isn't on Forvo, you can always ask someone to pronounce it for you on Rhinospike. Rhinospike is another helpful online language community that will let you connect to, and exchange audio files with, users from around the world.

I also recommend *Wiktionary.org,* as this collaborative online resource can prove quite useful for searching IPA pronunciation. Other than that, your own dictionary's phonetic transcriptions would most likely do

Practice Listening with Audio books, Podcasts and Videos

Audio books

Audio lessons can be quite helpful and convenient for anyone wishing to learn a foreign language. For this, I have a small product called "Learn French with Stories" that will help to improve your listening skills. It contains seven easy stories with an English glossary for difficult words, but more importantly, you can have the audio for free. It is currently a bestseller on Amazon. com, Amazon UK, Amazon Canada and Australia. Go check it out as soon as you can.

Other options, like librivox, are also available online. They have a very limited section in French, but it's free. This one is ideal for advanced learners.

Podcast:

Podcasts are increasing in popularity as a language learning tool. Below are some of the top French podcasts to subscribe to.

Coffee Break French is a great resource, no matter the level.

It is fun, informative, and highly encouraging. They also have a separate podcast called One Minute French with some very basic French lessons, in case you're under time-constraints.

Learn From By Podcast is another one you could try. The podcast features natural-sounding conversations about everyday matters followed by an analysis and discussion of the grammar and vocabulary used.

DailyFrenchPod combines a daily podcast, a variety of learning tools, and a large community of students & experts to practice with.

French Pod 101 has French language podcasts for all levels, from the absolute beginner to the advanced French language speaker. Each lesson offers a variety of language learning tools including dialogue, cultural insight and information about travelling and living in the country.

Journal en Francais Facile is also good. Though not for complete beginners, the podcast provides an easy dialogue and a transcript of the episodes.

Video:

Fluentu – this site offers videos to help you learn faster and promises to "bring language learning to life" through using entertaining content delivered in the form of varied videos.

Yabla – like fluentu, this is also an immersion site offering interactive videos to language learners. They have a really cool Smart Subtitle technology that you can put on slow play, access an integrated dictionary, and several other nifty features.

Apprendre tv5 monde – this site offers videos with quizzes and transcripts. These are categorised into levels.

Golden moustache also contains videos with perfect French subtitles for you to follow. You may view these at https://www. youtube.com/user/GoldenMoustacheVideo

  For more online resources, you can always drop by my site www.talkinfrench.com and check out our array of products that are guaranteed to help different kinds of learners.

BONUS 1 : Study Plan

Study Plan for Beginners

*T*his study plan is ideal for beginners who have no previous experience with French, or even those with a limited background in French.

How to use this guide

First of all, *congratulations on deciding to embark on a new journey*! I am as thrilled as you are with your new pursuit. To help you figure out how to use this study guide, here are some things you should understand before proceeding.

- **The frequency of study is categorized into different levels of *busy-ness***

This study plan is designed to accommodate your level of busy-ness. See below for the schedule break-downs.

1. **Ultra Busy** –. these are the *super-busy, running-around-all-day* kind of learners, those who can only allocate 15 – 20 minutes each day to studying. I value quality of learning over quantity, so that is better than nothing, right?

2. **Busy Bee** – these are the learners who are still quite busy but can spare 30 – 40 minutes daily to learn French.

3. **Slightly Busy** – these are the learners who can sneak in an hour per day to study French.

4. **Plenty of Time** – these are the learners who have the luxury to appropriate 2 hours every day to focus on French. In an ideal world, all language learners would be able to spare this much time.

Study Plan for Beginners

- **Monthly objectives**

Due to the differences in the lengths of time spent by each learner on studying daily, each learner type will have a different pace of learning. Therefore, the target number of grammar topics will vary. See the chart below for a guide on the monthly objectives.

Busy-ness level	Number of grammar topics per week	Number of topics per month
Ultra Busy	1 – 2	6 – 8
Busy Bee	2 – 3	8 – 12
Slightly Busy	3	12
Plenty of Time	4 – 5	15

- **Beginner level vocabulary topics**

To get you started, here is a list of the vocabulary topics you should focus on at this point in your learning journey. Use this list to guide you as you set the vocabulary foundation you will build your studies upon.

For the most extensive vocabulary list, grab a copy of the e-book "Improving French Vocabulary." It has a comprehensive list of vocabulary you will need, including the words on this list. You can also review this article for tips on how to efficiently memorize vocabulary.

- o Age
- o Appearances and Describing People
- o Asking for Directions/ Giving Directions
- o Asking for Favors
- o Clothing
- o Countable & Uncountable Nouns/ Numbers
- o Daily Routines
- o Days of the Week
- o Family
- o Feelings/ Emotions
- o Food
- o Greetings
- o Hobbies
- o Introductions
- o Jobs & Occupations
- o Making Plans
- o Months
- o Telling Time
- o Weather
- o Weekends

Study Plan for Beginners

- **Beginner level grammar topics**

   To guide you on which topics to focus on, here is a list of grammar topics for your level of learning. Grab a copy of the "Beginner's French Grammar e-book" as a resource.

o Les Salutations (greetings)
o Les Articles (articles)
o Le verbe "être"
o La negation (negation)
o Il y a (there is)
o Poser des questions (asking questions)
o Le présent simple (simple present)
o The Quick Way to Express Past, Present, and Future
o Expressing Causes and Results
o Directions and Locations
o Using Avoir in Perfect Tense (Passé Composé)
o Using être in Perfect Tense (Passé Composé)
o The Imperfect Tense
o Comparative and Superlative
o Possessive and Demonstrative Adjectives

o   Direct and Indirect Object Pronouns
o   Adverbs
o   Relative Pronoun (que/ that)
o   Numbers
o   Time, Duration, and Related Expressions

- **Resource materials**

Before you move on to the daily plan for the first 7 days, it is highly recommended that you download the free Talk in French learning package here:

http://www.talkinfrench.com/french-free-package.

It contains a wide range of resources that you can use to kick-start your learning. You can also find a lot of articles on talkin-french.com that are specifically designed for beginners. Explore those articles here.

Recommended e-books from Talk in French: You will need a good grammar book, such as those previously mentioned, as well as an extensive vocabulary book that you can still use even as you progress to higher learning levels. You can get the "Improving French Vocabulary" e-book now.

You can also purchase my French phrasebook with tons of great phrases that will help you sound like a natural French speaker. Get my French Phrasebook here.

The 7-Day Plan

Day 1: 1 hour

No matter how busy your schedule is, it is highly recommended that you allocate 1 hour to studying for the first day of your French language journey. Your first task is the following:

Start by studying pronunciation for 50 minutes

Get to know the different French alphabet sounds and their pronunciations, from the vowels to the consonants and the stress and accent marks. You can download the pronunciation guide here. It comes with a free mp3 as well so you can practice listening.

https://www.talkinfrench.com/download-pronunciation-guide-mp3.

Tackling pronunciation first is the most logical way to go about studying, since doing so will give your listening skills an immediate boost. You can learn to recognize words, which will make vocabulary easier to remember and give your reading and speaking skills an instant boost.

After studying pronunciation, follow it up with studying the **basic greetings** for 10 minutes. Try pronouncing the greetings using the rules you have just learned.

Day 2

TASKS	ULTRA BUSY (15-20 minutes per day)	BUSY BEE (30-40 minutes per day)	SLIGHT-LY BUSY (1 hour per day)	PLENTY OF TIME (2 hours per day)
Learn new vocabulary	5 minutes	10 minutes	15 minutes	30 minutes
Grammar lesson	10 minutes	20 minutes	20 minutes	40 minutes
Practice listening	5 minutes	10 minutes	15 minutes	20 minutes
Practice reading			10 minutes	10 minutes
Practice speaking (alternative writing)				20 minutes

Day 3

TASKS	ULTRA BUSY (15-20 minutes per day)	BUSY BEE (30-40 minutes per day)	SLIGHTLY BUSY (1 hour per day)	PLENTY OF TIME (2 hours per day)
Learn new vocabulary	5 minutes	10 minutes	10 minutes	30 minutes

Study Plan for Beginners

Grammar lesson	10 minutes	20 minutes	15 minutes	30 minutes
Practice listening			15 minutes	20 minutes
Practice reading				10 minutes
Practice speaking (alternative writing)	5 minutes	10 minutes	20 minutes	30 minutes

Day 4

TASKS	ULTRA BUSY (15-20 minutes per day)	BUSY BEE (30-40 minutes per day)	SLIGHTLY BUSY (1 hour per day)	PLENTY OF TIME (2 hours per day)
Learn new vocabulary	5 minutes	10 minutes	15 minutes	30 minutes
Grammar lesson	10 minutes	20 minutes	20 minutes	30 minutes
Practice listening			15 minutes	30 minutes
Practice reading	5 minutes	10 minutes	10 minutes	10 minutes

Practice speaking (alternative writing)				20 minutes

Day 5

TASKS	ULTRA BUSY (15-20 minutes per day)	BUSY BEE (30-40 minutes per day)	SLIGHTLY BUSY (1 hour per day)	PLENTY OF TIME (2 hours per day)
Learn new vocabulary	5 minutes	10 minutes	15 minutes	30 minutes
Grammar lesson	10 minutes	20 minutes	20 minutes	30 minutes
Practice listening	5 minutes	10 minutes	15 minutes	20 minutes
Practice reading			10 minutes	20 minutes
Practice speaking (alternative writing)				20 minutes

Study Plan for Beginners

Day 6: Review

TASKS	ULTRA BUSY (15-20 minutes per day)	BUSY BEE (30-40 minutes per day)	SLIGHTLY BUSY (1 hour per day)	PLENTY OF TIME (2 hours per day)
Review vocabulary	5- 10 minutes	10 minutes	15 minutes	20 minutes
Review grammar lesson	5- 10 minutes	20 minutes	20 minutes	30 minutes
Practice listening			10 minutes	20 minutes
Practice reading				20 minutes
Practice speaking (alternative writing)	5 minutes	10 minutes	15 minutes	30 minutes

Day 7: Rest (Watch a French movie or, even better, a TV series with French subtitles)

Repeat this schedule during the coming weeks until you learn all the grammar points and vocabulary topics for your level.

Since you are just starting out, it is important for you to begin strong and keep yourself motivated. To do that, 15 – 30 minutes of learning per day just won't cut it. However, I am aware that you likely have a busy schedule, so I have created a guide to help you continue learning at a successful rate.

Here is a recommended list of additional activities that you can weave into your daily routine. Take note that the time indicated is just a guide and you can change it to fit your lifestyle. Likewise, feel free to pick and choose among the suggested activities and stick to the ones that are the most fun for you. The important thing is to get French into your system to solidify a lasting learning habit.

Morning:

- **(6 am)** On your morning jog, listen to French techno music in **TuneIn** or **Spotify**. For starters, you can look for the album 1, 2, 3 Techno: Songs for Learning French. It has easy to follow songs that are perfect for beginners.

- **(8 am)** During your commute to work, listen to the Absolute Beginner podcast in **FrenchPod101** or season 1 of **Coffee Break French**. Talk In French will also be releasing a new podcast soon, so watch out for it!

Afternoon:

- **(2 pm)** While sipping coffee, take out your smartphone and sign in to **memrise.com**. Use the app to learn new vocabulary easily with its fun memory games. Some days you can also mix it up with **Anki**. You can decide which works best for you.

- **(3:30 pm)** Need a breather from all the hard work you are putting in at the office? Then it is definitely time for a social media break. Visit the Talk In French Facebook page and learn the word of the day. You can check it out on Instagram, too. Search for the account name @ talkinfrench.

- **(5 pm)** Head home while listening to French songs through **TuneIn Radio** or **Spotify.** There are tons of good French songs you can listen to from a variety of genres.

Evening:

- (**6 pm**) It is time for your daily study! Whether it is 20 minutes or 2 hours, make the most of it and learn as much as you can without pushing yourself past the limit. Learning should be fun, after all.

- (**9 pm**) It is time to relax and reflect on all of the knowledge you have gained during the day.

Note:

If you have found a native French speaker online (or a tutor) to practice speaking with, the schedule for your speaking practice will vary depending on which time zone you are in. Take into account the time difference and work out your schedule based on what works for you and your conversation partner. If you are in Australia, it could be during the evening while it is morning in France and most French-speaking countries; if you are in the US or Canada, it could be some time during the morning or early afternoon.

Study Plan for Intermediate Learners

*T*his study plan is ideal for learners who already have previous experience studying the French language but have not yet achieved proficiency.

Focus Areas

If you are an intermediate-level learner, you are most likely facing problems understanding native speakers or quickly translating in your head before you speak. To address these issues, this study plan will focus on enhancing your listening and writing skills.

Here is a list of priority vocabulary that you should tackle at your stage. For the most extensive list of vocabulary, grab a copy of the e-book Improving French Vocabulary. Covering 18,000 words, it includes a comprehensive list of the vocabulary you will need. Additional sources and descriptions are listed in the chart below. You can also review this article for tips on how to efficiently memorize vocabulary.

Chores	See vocabulary book	Adverbs of Degree	See vocabulary book
Colors	See vocabulary book	Adverbs of Frequency	See vocabulary book
Compara-tives	Here is a good article for compara-tives	Agree/ Dis-agree	See the article 50 French expressions for agreeing/dis-agreeing
Entertain-ment	See vocabulary book	Books & Reading	See vocabulary book

Study Plan for Intermediate Learners

Favorite Things	*See vocabulary book*	**Cooking**	*See vocabulary book*
Fruit/ Vegetables	Review fruits and veggies here	**Cultures**	*See vocabulary book*
Health	*See vocabulary book*	**Drinks**	*See vocabulary book*
Body Parts	*See vocabulary book*	**Environment**	*See vocabulary book*
Beauty & Physical Attractiveness	*See vocabulary book*	**Goals**	*See vocabulary book*
House/ Home	*See vocabulary book*	**Hopes, Dreams, & Wishes**	*See vocabulary book*
Likes and Dislikes	*See vocabulary book*	**In the Supermarket**	*See vocabulary book*
Movies	*See vocabulary book*	**Invitations (How to Invite)**	*See vocabulary book*
Nationalities	*See vocabulary book*	**Main Furniture and Home Kitchen/ Living Room/ Bathroom/ Bedroom**	Review material here.

Personality & Character	See common vocabulary here	**Buildings & Places**	*See vocabulary book*
Restaurants & Eating Out	See additional slang phrases for dining and drinking and vocabulary for food and drink	**Making a Complaint**	*See vocabulary book*
Seasons	Good material can be found here	**Music**	Vocabulary for music and dancing
Shapes	*See vocabulary book*	**Opposites**	*See vocabulary book*
Shopping	You can also check out the article Clothes and Footwear	**Parties**	*See vocabulary book*
Transportation	*See vocabulary book*	**Sports**	*See vocabulary book*
Vacations (Holidays)	*See vocabulary book*	**Summer Theme**	*See vocabulary book*

Enhancing your grammar knowledge can also help you in this stage of your learning. Brush up on your skills with the following list of priority topics. You can grab a copy of the e-book "French Grammar for Intermediate" to help you. Additional materials are included in the chart below.

Study Plan for Intermediate Learners

Imperative	Review it here: https://www.talkinfrench.com/learning-french-imperative-imperatif/
Cardinal Numbers vs. Ordinal Numbers	Review it here: https://www.talkinfrench.com/french-numbers
Telling the Time	Review it here: https://www.talkinfrench.com/tell-time-french/
The Weather	*See grammar book*
The Perfect Tense (Passé Composé) vs. The Imperfect Tense (Imparfait)	*See grammar book* *(French Beginner Grammar in 30 days from Talk in French)* *Chapter 10*
Simple Future Tense	*Intermediate's French Grammar in 30 days from Talk in French* *Chapter 6*
Placement of Adjective	Review it here: http://french.about.com/od/grammar/a/adjectives_4.htm
The Subjunctive Mood	Review it here: https://www.talkinfrench.com/5-things-need-know-french-subjunctive/ and here: https://www.talkinfrench.com/french-subjunctive-phrases/
Conditionals/ Conditional Tense (Passé Composé)	A supplementary article can be found here: https://www.talkinfrench.com/french-conditional-tense/

en and y	A quick guide can be found here: https:// www.talkinfrench.com/french-pronoun-en-y-use-grammar/
C'est and il est	Review it here: http://french.about.com/library/weekly/aa032500.htm
Stressed Pronouns	Check out this article: http://french.about.com/od/grammar/a/pronouns_stressed.htm
Order of Double Object	*Intermediate's French Grammar in 30 days from Talk in French* *Chapter 6*
Pronominal Verbs Reflexive Verbs	*Intermediate's French Grammar in 30 days from Talk in French* *Chapter 15*
Reciprocal Verb	*Intermediate's French Grammar in 30 days from Talk in French* *Chapter 13*
Idiomatic Pronominal Verbs	*Intermediate's French Grammar in 30 days from Talk in French* *Chapter 14*
Negation and Interrogation in Compound Tense	*Intermediate's French Grammar in 30 days from Talk in French* *Chapter 26*
Word Choice - Savoir or Connaître	*Intermediate's French Grammar in 30 days from Talk in French* *Chapter 27*

Coordinating Conjunctions	*Intermediate's French Grammar in 30 days from Talk in French* *Chapter 18*
Subordinating Conjunctions	*Intermediate's French Grammar in 30 days from Talk in French* *Chapter 17*

As a background, every language is divided into four different skills: reading and listening (receptive skills), and speaking and writing (productive skills). To be considered proficient in a language, you have to be adept at all four skills.

In order to tackle the different language skills mentioned, there are some prerequisites. These basic requirements will serve as the foundation for you to build your knowledge on.

Reading	**Listening**
– Pronunciation	– Pronunciation
– Vocabulary	– Knowledge of grammar
– Knowledge of grammar	– Understanding of conversational patterns and colloquial uses
– An understanding of conversational patterns	– Vocabulary (formal and informal)
	– Access to materials or native speakers to practice listening

Writing	Speaking
– Vocabulary	– Pronunciation
– Knowledge of grammar	– Low to mid-level grammar (to be able to get your message across)
	– Vocabulary (focus on the 1,500 high frequency words)

Recommended e-books from Talk in French: You will need a good grammar book, such as those previously mentioned, as well as an extensive vocabulary book that you can use even as you progress to higher learning levels. You can get the "Improving French Vocabulary" e-book now.

The 7-Day Plan

Before you move on to the daily plan for the first 7 days, it is highly recommended that you check out the intermediate level resources available on the Talk In French website. You should also consider following the steps suggested HERE and HERE on how you can form a listening habit that sticks. For variety, a good book to have is "Learn French with Stories," which you can get here.

For grammar, check out the e-book "French Grammar for Intermediate." For vocabulary, this is a good resource book to have: http://www.talkinfrench.com/french-vocabulary-ebook/.

Day 1: (1 hour)

Start by going through a refresher course for 45 minutes

Review pronunciation, grammar, and vocabulary here:

Study Plan for Intermediate Learners

https://www.talkinfrench.com/download-pronunciation-guide-mp3

Follow up with a listening practice for 15 minutes. Check out this link for a good resource that includes transcription:

http://www1.rfi.fr/lffr/statiques/accueil_apprendre.asp

Day 2: Reading

For day 2, do a little bit of reading. Visit this link for some good reading exercises:

http://www.bonjourdefrance.co.uk/learn-french-online/comprehension/exercices-elementary

Practice your listening skills by choosing one of the resources provided earlier. For vocabulary practice, list 20 – 30 words you encountered during your reading and listening exercise and learn their meanings. Practice speaking and pronouncing these words.

How busy are you?

Check out the chart below to determine the length of time you should allot for each task depending on your schedule. Of course, a longer amount of time (1 to 2 hours per day) is ideal. However, if you are busy, a good 20 – 40 minute session is enough to learn the essentials.

TASKS	ULTRA BUSY (15-20 minutes per day)	BUSY BEE (30-40 minutes per day)	SLIGHTLY BUSY (1 hour per day)	PLENTY OF TIME (2 hours per day)
Grammar lesson		10 minutes	10 minutes	10 minutes

Practice listening	5 minutes	10 minutes	10 minutes	20 minutes
Practice reading	5 minutes	5 minutes	15 minutes	30 minutes
Learn new vocabulary	5 minutes	5 minutes	10 minutes	15 minutes
Practice speaking				20 minutes
Practice writing	5 minutes	10 minutes	10 minutes	25 minutes

Day 3: Writing/ Speaking (If you can find a partner or tutor)

For day 3, it is time for a writing exercise! Think of a subject you are interested in and compose a short essay on the topic. Try to use some grammar points you recently learned, as well as 20 – 30 new vocabulary words, as you write.

How busy are you?

TASKS	ULTRA BUSY (15-20 minutes per day)	BUSY BEE (30-40 minutes per day)	SLIGHTLY BUSY (1 hour per day)	PLENTY OF TIME (2 hours per day)
Grammar lesson	5 minutes	10 minutes	10 minutes	10 minutes

Practice listening		5 minutes	5 minutes	20 minutes
Practice reading		5 minutes	5 minutes	10 minutes
Learn new vocabulary		10 minutes	10 minutes	20 minutes
Practice writing	15 minutes	30 minutes	20 minutes	20 minutes
Practice speaking			20 minutes	40 minutes

Day 4: Grammar

Choose a problem area in your grammar studies and focus on it. Here are some ideas for review: http://french.about.com/od/intgram/

How busy are you?

TASKS	ULTRA BUSY (15-20 minutes per day)	BUSY BEE (30-40 minutes per day)	SLIGHTLY BUSY (1 hour per day)	PLENTY OF TIME (2 hours per day)
Grammar lesson	15 minutes	15 minutes	30 minutes	50 minutes
Practice listening	5 minutes	5 minutes	5 minutes	15 minutes

Practice reading		5 minutes	5 minutes	10 minutes
Learn new vocabulary		10 minutes	10 minutes	15 minutes
Practice writing		5 minutes	10 minutes	10 minutes
Practice speaking				20 minutes

Day 5: Reading Comprehension

Focus on reading for day 5. Go to http://www.bonjourdefrance.co.uk/learn-french-online/comprehension/exercices-elementary and practice reading to improve your comprehension.

List 20 – 30 words you encountered during your reading exercise and learn their meanings. Practice speaking and pronouncing these words.

How busy are you?

TASKS	ULTRA BUSY (15-20 minutes per day)	BUSY BEE (30-40 minutes per day)	SLIGHTLY BUSY (1 hour per day)	PLENTY OF TIME (2 hours per day)
Grammar lesson		10 minutes	10 minutes	20 minutes
Practice listening	5 minutes	5 minutes	10 minutes	20 minutes

Practice reading	15 min-utes	15 minutes	20 minutes	40 minutes
Learn new vo-cabulary		10 minutes	10 minutes	15 minutes
Practice writing			10 minutes	20 minutes
Practice speaking				

Day 6: Focus on Listening.

On day 6, it is time to devote your time to listening. Listen to French podcasts, music, clips of conversations, or the live journal (http://www1.rfi.fr/lffr/statiques/accueil_apprendre.asp).

List 20 – 30 vocabulary words you heard, study their meanings, and use them in sentences of your own.

How busy are you?

TASKS	ULTRA BUSY	BUSY BEE	SLIGHTLY BUSY	PLENTY OF TIME
	(15-20 minutes per day)	(30-40 minutes per day)	(1 hour per day)	(2 hours per day)
Grammar lesson				
Practice listening	15 min-utes	15 min-utes	20 minutes	40 minutes

Read the tran-scripts		5 minutes	10 minutes	20 minutes
Learn new vo-cabulary	5 min-utes	10 min-utes	10 minutes	20 minutes
Practice speaking		10 min-utes	20 minutes	20 minutes
Practice writing				20 minutes

Day 7: Recap or Practice Speaking With Someone.

Review everything you have learned in the last week, and treat yourself to a good French movie!

ULTRA BUSY	BUSY BEE	SLIGHTLY BUSY	PLENTY OF TIME
Set aside at least 25 minutes for review	Set aside around 50 minutes for review	Allocate around 75 minutes for review	Allocate the en-tire 2 hours, plus an additional 20 minutes, for review

Study Plan for Advanced Learners

*T*his study plan is ideal for learners who have already developed an advanced level of proficiency in French. You can Be considered an Advanced learner if You:

- Can hold conversations for an extended period of time and can write lengthy texts.
- Can distinguish between formal and informal speech.
- Still make occasional mistakes in grammar but have little difficulty communicating about everyday topics and specialized subjects.
- Have a strong grasp of French pronunciation, though you do not yet sound like a native speaker.

If you have already reached this level, *great job*! You are well on your way to fluency. Continue studying at a steady pace and keep your motivation intact.

Focus Areas

At this stage, the most common trouble areas for learners are:

- Prepositions (à / de)
- Subjunctive
- Conditional
- Expressions
- Pronominal Verbs (especially idiomatic)
- Pronunciation (especially understanding French rhythm)
- Indefinite and Partitive Articles (De, du, de la, or des?)
- Verbs with Prepositions
- C'est vs Il est
- The different uses of *Le*
- Indefinite French

Study Plan for Advanced Learners

- Impersonal French
- Reflexive vs. Object Pronouns
- Agreement

As an advanced French learner, your focus should be on these troublesome areas. Aside from that, a wider vocabulary is also expected for you to move forward in your learning.

Recommended e-books from Talk in French: To expand your vocabulary, listed below are some priority vocabulary topics for you to focus on. For the most extensive list of vocabulary words, grab a copy of the e-book Improving French Vocabulary. It covers 18,000+ words and all the vocabulary that you will need.

Annoying Habits / Bad habits	Book Review (Report)	Architecture	Addiction
Birthdays	Dieting	Body Language	Advertising
Countries & Capitals	Dreams, Daydreams, & Nightmares	Celebrities & Famous People	Creative Writing
Customs & Traditions	Fashion	Crime	Disability
Dating	Healthy Lifestyle	Fair / Not Fair / Unfair	Discrimination
Planning a Trip	Idioms	Fairy Tale & Fantasy	Drinking Alcohol
Exhibits / Museums	Internet	Government	Gambling

Fears & Phobias	Money	History	Gender Roles
Gardening	New Year's Resolutions	Honesty	Smoking
Machines	Dream House	Humor	Socializing
Manners	Making Promises	Inventions	Tolerance
Nature	Rules & Taboos	Jokes	Racism
Part-time Jobs	Vegetarianism	Lies / Lying	Charity / Volunteer Work
Pets	Writing a Letter	Politics	Natural Disasters
Playground	Gestures	Police, Detectives, & Prison	Poverty
Senses	Make-up	Prejudice	Retirement
Friendship	Science	Punishment	Flowers
Tools	Religion	Job Interview	Animals
Toys	Art	Radio	
Visiting a Doctor	Relationships	Culture Shock	

Further enhancing your grammar knowledge can also help you at this stage of your learning process. Brush up on your skills

Study Plan for Advanced Learners

with the following list of priority topics.

Advanced Grammar Topics	Resources
Prepositions Par, Pour and En	Review par here: http://french.about.com/od/grammar/a/preposition_par.htm, Review pour here: http://french.about.com/od/grammar/a/preposition_pour.htm Review en here: http://french.about.com/od/grammar/a/preposition_en.htm
Prepositions à and de	Review à here: http://french.about.com/od/grammar/a/preposition_a.htm Review de here: http://french.about.com/library/prepositions/bl_prep_de.htm Review here: http://french.about.com/library/prepositions/bl_prep_a_vs_de.htm
Verbs with Prepositions de and à	http://french.about.com/library/prepositions/bl_prep_a_vs_de2.htm
Express the Objective	*Intermediate's French Grammar in 30 days from Talk in French* *Chapter 24*
Express Opposition and Restriction	*Intermediate's French Grammar in 30 days from Talk in French* *Chapter 25*
The Three Forms of 'If' in French	*Intermediate's French Grammar in 30 days from Talk in French* *Chapter 7*
Exclamation Sentence	http://french.about.com/od/grammar/a/exclamations.htm

The Present Participle	http://french.about.com/od/grammar/a/pre-sentparticiple.htm

Using c'est.. que / qui Sentence Structure for Emphasis	http://french.about.com/od/pronunciation/a/tonicaccent.htm
The Infinitive Mood	http://french.about.com/od/infinitive/
The Pluperfect	Review these pages: http://www.talkinfrench.com/french-pluperfect/ and http://french.about.com/od/grammar/a/pastperfect.htm
Impersonal Verb	http://french.about.com/od/grammar/a/impersonal-verbs.htm
The Passive Voice	http://french.about.com/od/grammar/a/pas-sivevoice.htm
The Future Perfect (Anterior Future)	http://french.about.com/od/grammar/a/fu-tureperfect.htm
The Historical Past Tense (Simple Past)	Review these pages: https://www.talkin-french.com/french-past-simple-passe-simple/ http://www.french-linguistics.co.uk/grammar/passe_simple.shtml and http://french.about.com/od/grammar/a/passesimple.htm
The Past Subjunctive	http://french.about.com/od/grammar/a/past-subjunctive.htm

Study Plan for Advanced Learners

Special Expressions with Subjunctive and Indicative	https://www.talkinfrench.com/french-subjunctive-phrases/
Modal Verbs	Visit these pages: https://www.talkinfrench.com/french-modal-verbs/ and http://french.about.com/od/grammar/a/french-modal-verbs.htm
Sequence of Tenses - Concordance des temps	http://french.about.com/library/weekly/bl-concordancedestemps.htm

Here are additional (super) advanced topics that you can also work on. At this point, however, it is still completely optional.

Double Negation	http://french.about.com/od/grammar/a/negation_double.htm
Indirect Speech	http://french.about.com/library/weekly/aa031100i.htm
French Causative - Le Causatif	http://french.about.com/od/grammar/a/causative.htm
French Faux Adjectives ~ Adjectifs Occasionnels	http://french.about.com/od/grammar/a/adjectives_faux.htm
French Expletive Ne - Formal French	http://french.about.com/od/grammar/a/negation_form_2.htm
French Passive Infinitive	http://french.about.com/od/grammar/a/passiveinf.htm

As a quick background, every language is divided into four different skills: reading and listening (receptive skills), and speaking and writing (productive skills). To be considered fluent in a certain language, you have to be adept at all four skills.

In order to tackle the different language skills mentioned, there are some prerequisites. These basic requirements serve as the foundation on which you should build your knowledge. As an advanced learner, a strong knowledge of the fundamentals for each skill is necessary.

Reading	**Listening**
• Pronunciation	• Pronunciation
• Vocabulary	• Knowledge of grammar
• Knowledge of grammar	• Understanding of conversational patterns and colloquial use
• An understanding of conversational patterns	• Vocabulary (formal and informal)
	• Access to materials or native speakers to practice listening
Writing	**Speaking**
• Vocabulary	• Pronunciation
• Knowledge of grammar	• Grammar
	• Vocabulary
	• Access to native speakers to practice speaking

Study Plan for Advanced Learners

Materials and Resources

For advanced learners, the key to moving forward with your studies is to focus on acquiring more vocabulary and expressions, and to strengthen your knowledge of more complicated grammar topics. Make sure to browse the available materials in TalkInFrench.com created specifically for advanced learners like you. To exponentially increase your vocabulary, you can also check out the most comprehensive vocabulary e-book in the market, covering 18,000+ translated French words on 50 topics.

To help you sound more like a native speaker, brush up on your colloquial phrases and slang words. You can check out some excellent material here.

The 7-Day Plan

Day 1: (1 hour)
Start by going through a refresher course for 45 minutes

Review grammar and vocabulary and take stock of all that you have learned so far. Do a recap, focusing on any difficult points you might have encountered (see common areas listed in the beginning of this study plan); focus on those topics for your review.

Follow up with an **immersion activity for 15 minutes**. Stream French songs, listen to French podcasts, or watch a French TV series. You can find other good reading resources for advanced learners here: http://french.about.com/od/advlist/.

Day 2:

For day 2, it is time to work on improving your grammar. Review one of the grammar topics listed above.

How busy are you?

Check out the chart below to see the length of time you should allot for each task depending on your schedule. Of course, a longer amount of time (1 to 2 hours per day) is ideal. However, if you are busy, a good 20 to 40 minute session is enough to absorb the essentials.

TASKS	ULTRA BUSY (15-20 minutes per day)	BUSY BEE (30-40 minutes per day)	SLIGHTLY BUSY (1 hour per day)	PLENTY OF TIME (2 hours per day)
Grammar review	15 minutes	30 minutes	40 minutes	45 minutes
Practice listening				15 minutes
Practice reading	5 minutes	10 minutes	20 minutes	15 minutes
Learn new vocabulary				15 minutes
Practice speaking (For example: form sentences using the subjunctive/conditional)				30 minutes

Day 3:

Study Plan for Advanced Learners

For day 3, it is time to focus on sounding better and mastering French conversations. Listen to conversational French podcasts and practice speaking with a native French speaker. If you do not have a regular conversation partner at this point, you can visit sites such as *Italki* or *Interpals* to find one.

How busy are you?

TASKS	ULTRA BUSY (15-20 minutes per day)	BUSY BEE (30-40 minutes per day)	SLIGHTLY BUSY (1 hour per day)	PLENTY OF TIME (2 hours per day)
Practice listening	5 minutes	10 minutes	20 minutes	40 minutes
Practice writing				20 minutes (learn colloquial phrases)
Practice speaking	15 minutes	30 minutes	40 minutes	50 minutes
Read supplementary material / Learn new vocabulary				10 minutes (review liaisons)

Day 4:

For day 4, let's put the spotlight on prepositions. Study the prepositions Par, Pour, and En, as well as de and à.

How busy are you?

TASKS	ULTRA BUSY (15-20 minutes per day)	BUSY BEE (30-40 minutes per day)	SLIGHTLY BUSY (1 hour per day)	PLENTY OF TIME (2 hours per day)
Grammar review	15 minutes	30 minutes	40 minutes	45 minutes
Practice listening				15 minutes
Practice reading				15 minutes
Learn new vocabulary				15 minutes
Practice writing (form sentences using prep- ositions)	5 minutes	10 minutes	20 minutes	30 minutes

Day 5:

Increase your vocabulary by memorizing sets of vocabulary words and phrases that you have not mastered yet. See the vocabulary priority topics listed above.

How busy are you?

TASKS	ULTRA BUSY (15-20 minutes per day)	BUSY BEE (30-40 minutes per day)	SLIGHT-LY BUSY (1 hour per day)	PLENTY OF TIME (2 hours per day)
Learn new vo-cabulary	20 minutes	30 min-utes	40 min-utes	80 minutes
Practice reading		10 min-utes	20 min-utes	
Practice speaking				40 minutes

Day 6:

On day 6, it is time to devote your time to reading and writing. Improve your comprehension by reading somewhat complicated material of your choice and follow it up by writing a lengthy essay about your opinion on the topic.

How busy are you?

TASKS	ULTRA BUSY (15-20 minutes per day)	BUSY BEE (30-40 minutes per day)	SLIGHTLY BUSY (1 hour per day)	PLENTY OF TIME (2 hours per day)
Practice reading	10 minutes	15 minutes	20 minutes	60 minutes
Practice writing	10 minutes	25 minutes	40 minutes	60 minutes

Day 7: Recap

Review everything you have learned in the last week, and treat yourself to a French movie!

ULTRA BUSY	BUSY BEE	SLIGHTLY BUSY	PLENTY OF TIME
Set aside at least 25 minutes for review	Set aside around 50 minutes for review	Allocate around 75 minutes for review	Allocate the entire 2 hours, plus an additional 20 minutes, for review

Study Plan to Improve Speaking and Listening Comprehension

Many French learners have trouble speaking and listening. If you have a particular weakness in:

- Translating your thoughts or forming French sentences on the fly, and
- Understanding conversational French as spoken by native speakers,

then this study plan is definitely for you!

Recommended e-books from Talk in French:

The most complete Slang e-book available: http://www.talkin-french.com/product/french-slang-ebook/

To improve your listening comprehension: http://www.talkin-french.com/product/short-stories-french/

Focus Areas

For learners like you who are having a bit of trouble in the areas of speaking and listening, it is important that you focus on expanding your vocabulary. Spend a lot of time learning new words and their correct pronunciations, and practice using these in sentences with a study buddy who can correct your mistakes for you.

Below is the list of vocabulary you should prioritize at this point. For the most extensive list of vocabulary, grab a copy of the e-book "Improving French Vocabulary." It has all of the vocabulary you need. Additional sources and descriptions are included in the chart below. You can also review this article for tips on how to efficiently memorize vocabulary.

Study Plan to Improve Speaking and Listening Comprehension

False Cognate and True Cognate	Learn this to give your vocabulary an immediate boost
Adjectives	Check out this article of the 129 most common adjectives, and this article for a quick refresher on adjectives
Adverbs	Here is a simple refresher on adverbs
Daily Routine	Aside from the e-book, you can also check out this article on Daily Routine
Expressions	Refer to the e-book "365 Days of French Expressions"
Slang words	Refer to the e-book "French Slang"
Work	Aside from the vocabulary e-book, you can also refer to the article 30 Essential Work-related Words
Hobbies/ Sports	*See vocabulary book*
Cinema	Additional material can be found in this article on Cinema vocabulary
Reading	*See vocabulary book*
Express Opinion	Check out the article French Essay Phrases
Express Disagreement/ Agreement (articles)	See the article 50 French expressions for agreeing/disagreeing

Study Plan to Improve Speaking and Listening Comprehension

Express Taste	*See vocabulary book*
Social Media and Technology	A helpful article can be found <u>here</u>
Making Plans	*See vocabulary book*
Previous Trips/ Past Experiences	*See vocabulary book*
Shopping (clothes/ market)	You can also check out the article <u>Clothes and Footwear</u>
Restaurants	Check out this article on <u>French slang words for dining and drinking</u> and vocabulary for <u>food and drink</u>
Buying Tickets	*See vocabulary book*
Describe Things	Learn to describe shapes, sizes, colors, etc.
Making Appointments	*See vocabulary book*
Complain/ Claim Something	*See vocabulary book*
Ask Someone to Clarify	*See vocabulary book*
Filler/ Connectors	See bonus material

Enhancing your grammar knowledge can also help you in this stage of your learning. Brush up on your skills with the following list of priority topics.

Study Plan to Improve Speaking and Listening Comprehension

Pronunciation Rules for Liaisons	A quick review: https://www.talkinfrench.com/french-liaison/
Asking Questions	Here is a handy guide to use as a refresher
Present Tense for Irregular Verbs	Here are flashcards: http://www.cram.com/flashcards/french-irregular-verbs-present-tense-374818
Review Passé Composé vs Imparfait	Review it here: http://french.about.com/od/grammar/a/pasttenses.htm
Placement of Adjectives	Review it here: http://french.about.com/od/grammar/a/adjectives_4.htm
Homophones	Here is a helpful guide: http://french.about.com/od/vocabulary/a/homophones.htm
Informal Grammar	Visit this link: http://french.about.com/od/grammar/a/informal.htm
French Pronouns	Visit this link: http://french.about.com/od/pronouns/
French Conjunctions ~ Les Conjonctions	Here is a good review article: https://www.talkinfrench.com/french-conjunctions/
c'est vs il est	Review it here: http://french.about.com/library/weekly/aa032500.htm

Study Plan to Improve Speaking and Listening Comprehension

Prepositions	Check out http://french.about.com/library/weekly/aa010800.htm
Placement of Adverbs	Check out the bonus audio and vocabulary list
Conditional for Verbs for Requesting Something	Review it here: https://www.talkinfrench.com/french-conditional-tense/
Impersonal Pronouns	Here is review material: http://french.about.com/od/grammar/a/pronouns_2.htm
Subjunctive for Specific Situations	This covers the 10 most common verbs
Pronominal Verbs	Idiomatic in particular
en and y	A quick guide can be found here: https://www.talkinfrench.com/french-pronoun-en-y-use-grammar/
The Quick Way to Express Past, Present, and Future	Review it here: https://www.talkinfrench.com/french-tenses-made-easy/
Direct and Indirect Object Pronouns	Review material here: https://www.talkinfrench.com/french-direct-indirect-speech/
Numbers	Brush up on your French numbers here: https://www.talkinfrench.com/french-numbers/

Stressed Pro-nouns	Check out this article: http://french.about. com/od/grammar/a/pronouns_stressed. htm

As a bit of background, every language is divided into four different skills: reading and listening (receptive skills), and speaking and writing (productive skills). To be considered proficient in a language, you have to be adept at all four skills.

In order to tackle the different language skills mentioned, there are some prerequisites. These basic requirements serve as the foundation for you to build your knowledge on. To complete your studies and reach fluency, a strong knowledge of the fundamentals for each skill is necessary.

Reading	**Listening**
<ul><li>Pronunciation</li><li>Vocabulary</li><li>Knowledge of grammar</li><li>An understanding of conversational patterns</li></ul>	<ul><li>Pronunciation</li><li>Knowledge of grammar</li><li>Understanding of conversational patterns and colloquial uses</li><li>Vocabulary (formal and informal)</li><li>Access to materials or native speakers to practice listening</li></ul>

Study Plan to Improve Speaking and Listening Comprehension

Writing	Speaking
• Vocabulary • Knowledge of grammar	• Pronunciation • Low- to mid-level grammar (to be able to get your message across) • Vocabulary • Access to native speakers to practice speaking

The 7-Day Plan

Before you move on to the daily plan for the first 7 days, it is highly recommended that you have access to a native French speaker. A practice partner will help you master conversational French, plus you will have somebody to point your grammatical mistakes out to you.

Check out some options below:

- ***Interpals*** is the website you need if you are looking for someone to practice French with.

- ***Italki*** is a social networking and educational website for language learners. You can use the website to practice writing and receive corrections from native speakers, as well as find private teachers and native speakers to speak French with.

- ***Couchsurfing*** is another social networking website you can use to further your French studies. Couchsurfing is a community of travelers who regularly organize meetings; chances are, there is probably one near you. These meetings are great opportunities to meet French speakers with whom you can practice.

- ***Meetup.com*** is a website with 21 million members whose goal is to help people organize themselves into groups and communities. Here, you can find lots of language exchange meetings for you to take part in.

To help you sound more like a native speaker, brush up on your colloquial phrases and slang words. You can check out good material for this here.

You can also brush up on your listening skills with a book of stories as well as by listening to conversational French on podcasts like Learn French By Podcast, French Voices, and season 4 of <u>Coffee Break French.</u> Other options include streaming <u>French songs</u> and watching a <u>French TV series</u>.

Now, for the daily plan.

Day 1: Review Pronunciation

Spend half an hour on the first day focusing on pronunciation. For a refresher, download this pronunciation guide that comes with audio files: https://www.talkinfrench.com/download-pronunciation-guide-mp3

As mentioned earlier, it would be ideal at this point for you to find someone who can help you improve your pronunciation.

The remaining 30 minutes should be focused on memorizing new vocabulary. Check out the vocabulary priority list above for specific topics to focus on.

Day 2:

Two words: active listening. Get inspired with an article on the Talk in French website that discusses how to practice your listening skills effectively. Read it here: https://www.talkinfrench.com/practice-listening-french/

To make your listening practice as efficient as possible, list 20 – 30 new vocabulary words gathered from your listening session and study those as well.

How busy are you?

Check out the chart below to determine the length of time you should allot for each task depending on your schedule. Of course, a longer amount of time (1 to 2 hours per day) is ideal. However, if you are busy, a good 20 – 40 minute session is enough to practice the essentials.

TASKS	ULTRA BUSY (15-20 minutes per day)	BUSY BEE (30-40 minutes per day)	SLIGHTLY BUSY (1 hour per day)	PLENTY OF TIME (2 hours per day)
Practice listening	20 minutes Listen to the listening exercises at Talkin-French.com	40 minutes Listen to the listening exercises at Talkin-French.com and a podcast	1 hour Listen to: · Listening exercises · Podcast · French songs	2 hours divided into: · Listening exercises · Podcast · French songs · Audio books

Day 3:

It is time to practice speaking, first on your own. Practice commonly used phrases using a good phrasebook like this one, which also has an audiobook counterpart: http://www.talkinfrench.com/product/french-expressions.

Imitate the words and phrases and record yourself speaking. Replay the words until the sounds begin to flow effortlessly.

How busy are you?

TASKS	ULTRA BUSY (15-20 minutes per day)	BUSY BEE (30-40 minutes per day)	SLIGHTLY BUSY (1 hour per day)	PLENTY OF TIME (2 hours per day)
Practice listening		10 minutes	20 minutes	30 minutes

Practice speaking	20 minutes	30 minutes	40 minutes	60 minutes
Practice writing				20 minutes
Read supplementary material				10 minutes (review liaisons)

Day 4:

For day 4, work on mastering French conversations by reviewing vocabulary and grammar.

How busy are you?

TASKS	ULTRA BUSY (15-20 minutes per day)	BUSY BEE (30-40 minutes per day)	SLIGHTLY BUSY (1 hour per day)	PLENTY OF TIME (2 hours per day)
Vocabulary	15 minutes	30 minutes	40 minutes	60 minutes
Grammar	5 minutes	10 minutes	20 minutes	60 minutes

Day 5:

Increase your colloquial vocabulary by memorizing colloquial phrases and slang words. Click here for a sample of good material to use. It contains audio that you can listen to as well.

How busy are you?

TASKS	ULTRA BUSY (15-20 minutes per day)	BUSY BEE (30-40 minutes per day)	SLIGHT-LY BUSY (1 hour per day)	PLENTY OF TIME (2 hours per day)
Practice listening	5 minutes	10 minutes	15 minutes	20 minutes
Learn new vocabulary	20 minutes	20 minutes	30 minutes	60 minutes
Practice speaking		10 minutes	15 minutes	40 minutes

Day 6:

Call up your French conversation partner and spend an entire session practicing all the new vocabulary, grammar, and colloquial phrases you have learned from the previous days.

How busy are you?

TASKS	ULTRA BUSY (15-20 minutes per day)	BUSY BEE (30-40 minutes per day)	SLIGHTLY BUSY (1 hour per day)	PLENTY OF TIME (2 hours per day)

Prac-tice speak-ing	20 minutes	40 minutes	60 minutes	120 min-utes

Day 7: Recap

Review everything you have learned in the last week and treat yourself to a good French movie!

ULTRA BUSY	BUSY BEE	SLIGHTLY BUSY	PLENTY OF TIME
Spend at least 25 minutes on review	Spend around 50 minutes on review	Allocate around 75 minutes to review	Allocate the entire 2 hours, plus an additional 20 minutes, to review.

Bonus 2: Audio and PDF.

Additional bonus material (including audio) can be found by following these instructions:

How to download the MP3

Audio download instructions

- Copy and paste this link into your browser: http: https://www.talkinfrench.com/bonus-fluent-french/

- Click on the book cover. It will take you to a Dropbox folder containing each individual file. (If you're not familiar with what Dropbox is or how it works, don't panic, it just a storage facility.)

- Click the DOWNLOAD button in the Dropbox folder located in the upper right portion of your screen. A box may pop up asking you to sign in to Dropbox. Simply click, "No thanks, continue to download" under the sign in boxes. (If you have a Dropbox account, you can choose to save it to your own Dropbox so you have access anywhere via the internet.)

- The files you have downloaded will be saved in a .zip file. Note: This is large file. Don't try opening it until your browser tells you that it has completed the download successfully (usually a few minutes on a broadband connection but if your connection is unreliable, it could take 10 to 20 minutes).

- The files will be in your "downloads" folder unless you have changed your settings. Extract them from the folder and save them to your computer or copy to your preferred devices, et voilà ! You can now listen to the audio anytime, anywhere.

Additional instructions for iOS users

<u>How to download the MP3</u>

Talk in French products are completely compatible with all iOS devices but due to the limited control of the file system in Apple devices, you'll first need to download the files to your computer. After following the download instructions above you will need to:

1. **Import the file in iTunes.** (To make sure the files are copied to your internal library, go to iTunes > Edit>Preferences and click on the Advanced tab. Make sure they get transferred into the correct iTunes folder by checking the destination in the "iTunes Media folder location" box.) Then, in iTunes, select File > Add Folder to Library. Navigate to the folder where you placed the audio files. Then, highlight the folder and click, "Select Folder." Your files will be copied into your iTunes Media Library and will appear in your Music application under the artist, "Talk in French."

2. **Sync your iPad/iPhone with iTunes/iCloud.** You can now sync your device using iTunes or iCloud

3. **Questions?** If you have questions on downloading the book to your iOS device I recommend this YouTube video: https://www.youtube.com/watch?v=a_1VDD9KJhc? (You can skip the over 1 minute and 20 seconds.)

Do you have any problems downloading the audio?

If you have thoroughly reviewed the download instructions and are still having difficulty with the download, please send an email to contact@talkinfrench.com. I'll do my best to assist you!

Thank you. Merci.

Frederic

I am here to help!

I adore my language and culture and would love to share it with you.

Should you have any questions regarding my book, the French language and culture, or technical issues, I am happy to answer them. You can contact me via email or through the Talk in French Facebook page.

Email: Frederic@talkinfrench.com
Facebook: facebook.com/talkinfrench

ABOUT THE AUTHOR

*F*rédéric BIBARD is the founder of Talkinfrench.com. He helps motivated learners to improve their French and create a learning habit.

Visit his website: talkinfrench.com

Made in the USA
Columbia, SC
19 September 2019